# REFLECTIONS ON RAYBURN

# REFLECTIONS ON RAYBURN

*James W. Riddlesperger Jr.*
*Anthony Champagne*
*Editors*

A Joint Project of the Center for Texas Studies at TCU
*and* TCU Press / Fort Worth, TX

Copyright © 2017 by James W. Riddlesperger Jr. and Anthony Champagne

*Library of Congress Cataloging-in-Publication Data*

Names: Jim Wright Symposium (14th : 2015 : Fort Worth, Tex.), author. | Riddlesperger, James W., Jr., 1953- editor. | Champagne, Anthony, editor. | Wright, Jim, 1922–2015. | Texas Christian University, sponsoring body.

Title: Reflections on Rayburn / James W. Riddlesperger, Jr. and Anthony Champagne, editors.

Description: Fort Worth, Texas : TCU Press, [2017] | The 2015 Jim Wright Symposium was dedicated to the 75th anniversary of Sam Rayburn becoming Speaker of the House.

Identifiers: LCCN 2017045049 (print) | LCCN 2017048883 (ebook) | ISBN 9780875656823 | ISBN 9780875656700 | ISBN 9780875656700?(alk. paper)

Subjects: LCSH: Rayburn, Sam, 1882–1961^Congresses. | United States. Congress. House—Biography. | Legislators—United States—Biography. | United States—Politics and government—1901–1953. | Texas—Politics and government—1865–1950.

Classification: LCC E748.R24 (ebook) | LCC E748.R24 J56 2017 (print) | DDC 328.73/092 [B]—dc23

LC record available at https://urldefense.proofpoint.com/v2/url?u=https-3A__lccn.loc.gov_2017045049&d=DwIFAg&c=7Q-FWLBTAxn3T_E3HWrzGYJrC4RvUoWDrzTlitGRH_A&r=O2eiy819IcwTGuw-vrBGiVdm-hQxMh2yxeggw9qlTUDE&m=QMr-kKUVz_9-1AugmofqGuMeAF1ordAQoMAMk92WS7Q&s=HFqyja2svplLEpOpgR3lDu54KlGTu5Kn_ELTSov1swk&e=

TCU Press
TCU Box 298300
Fort Worth, Texas 76129
817.257.7822
www.prs.tcu.edu
To order books: 1.800.826.8911

Text and cover design by David Timmons

# Contents

Speaker Sam Rayburn, seated, with Jim Wright standing. *Courtesy Jim Wright Collection, TCU.*

1

# Some Called Him Mr. Sam

## *Sam Rayburn Remembered*

Former House Speaker Jim Wright

Most House colleagues were saying "Mr. Speaker." Some still called him "Mister Sam," and nobody asked of whom it was they spoke in that long middle period of the twentieth century. Samuel Taliaferro Rayburn was not only the longest-serving presiding officer in the history of the US Congress, I believe that he also was the most effective leader and the most unhesitatingly trusted. Mr. Rayburn's back-scenes help and advice were sought by presidents of both parties and treasured by veteran lawmakers.

• • •

Among the vignettes of remembrance that come rushing back at the mention of Mr. Rayburn's name is an event that occurred on January 6, 1955. It was on the occasion of President Dwight D. Eisenhower's third annual State of the Union message. The president unexpectedly began his speech by mentioning that it was January 6 and the seventy-second birthday of the venerable Speaker of the House, and publicly wished for Mr. Rayburn many happy returns of the day.

Instantly, the crowd that filled the House chamber was on its feet, noisily cheering, whistling, and stamping its feet and clapping its hands in a reverberating approval of the Speaker. Visitors in the galleries could not distinguish Republican from Democrat.

• • •

The noisy ovation persisted until Mr. Rayburn, faintly blushing, rose from his seat behind the dais and gently rapped his gravel to restore order.

• • •

One of my primary duties after my first election to Congress was to stop by and pay my respects to the Speaker. It was there that I learned how willing he was to share his wisdom.

In the process of expressing my desire to be a team player, I mentioned that I'd thought of applying for assignment to the House Foreign Affairs Committee.

Hoping to enlist his aid in fulfilling my ambition, I mentioned my long-held ambition to make a lasting contribution to world peace.

The old gentleman calmly replied, "That's a wonderful ambition, but I'd hate to see you disappointed. Have you considered how little influence the House Committee exerts in those matters?"

Rayburn explained the powers held exclusively by the Senate—ratification of treaties and the making of ambassadors, and how the assertion of these powers often fairly monopolizes the field of congressional initiative in foreign policy.

Then he contrasted the opportunities for almost immediate and visible service to the citizens of one's community and state through an active House Committee known as Public Works. There was an available vacancy for a Texan on that committee, he said, and added that he'd hoped I might like to seize that opportunity and become an effective advocate for Texas and other areas needing approval for worthy projects.

Twenty-two years later, in 1977, I was in place by seniority to be the next chairman of Public Works until colleagues whom I'd assisted and befriended were urging me to seek the post of House majority leader. This post, second in influence to that of the Speaker, was just being vacated by Tip O'Neill, who was stepping up to be Speaker. I thought back over those two decades to that day in Rayburn's office and thanked my long-deceased benefactor for his good advice.

• • •

Just as Sam Rayburn's personal popularity crossed party lines, so did his friendship and respect for members of both parties.

Mr. Sam's personal admiration for his opposite number in the House leadership, Rep. Joe Martin of Massachusetts, the elected minority leader, was well known.

The Democratic Speaker would tolerate in his presence no criticism of Republican Martin. I've heard Rayburn say, "If Joe tells you something, you can absolutely put it in the bank!"

One telling incident occurred following two brief two-year intervals in which Republicans had enjoyed a temporary majority. During those short periods Martin had moved his private office accoutrements into the space reserved for the Speaker and his staff, while the small Rayburn group had to move into the minority leader's quarters. After the second such two-year switch, Rayburn learned how attached his opposite number had become to the view from the west window of his temporary quarters, encompassing the long, grassy mall, past the monuments to the Lincoln Memorial and the National Cemetery across the Potomac River.

Learning of his rival's powerful deep personal regret at having to abandon this cherished treasure for a second time, Rayburn approached Joe Martin personally and said, "Joe, I'm tired of this moving back and forth. Why don't you and I just stay right where we are with our little private offices and devote our time to legislating instead of shuffling our books and papers around?" Needless to say, the Massachusetts Republican was personally thrilled in spite of his party's loss of its brief House majority.

• • •

Rayburn, with all his strong sense of fairness to the opposing party, made no secret of his own convictions and affiliations. "Without prefix, without suffix, and without apology, I am a Democrat!" he would say whenever asked.

As much as he respected the presidency and gave honor to presidents of both parties, he insistently upheld the constitutional equality between the branches of our government and stubbornly refused ever to consider the Congress in any way subordinate to the presidency. Asked toward the end of his career "how many presidents he'd served under," Rayburn crisply replied: "I've never served under any. I've served with eight."

But the solemn constitutional demands of the presidential office were never minimized in Rayburn's view. Early on, he had developed a close personal friendship with Vice President Harry Truman, and the two men were enjoying a private visit in a small office in the Capitol just off the House Chamber at the time President Roosevelt was pronounced dead in Georgia. The telephone rang, and the two men learned that the White House was calling for Vice President Truman. Rayburn watched as his friend acknowledged, listened, and then fell deadly silent, his face ashen and bearing a horrified expression.

No words were necessary. Both men knew instinctively. The president was dead, and Vice President Harry Truman was automatically occupying the office. Truman's first words were an exhausted cry:

"Sam, I can't do it!"

"Mr. President," the Speaker replied with solemnity, "you've gotta do it!"

• • •

Perhaps the most convincing proof of the unparalleled personal respect in which Sam Rayburn was held by his colleagues—Democrats and Republicans alike—occurred during World War II. With the highly secret scientific discovery of nuclear energy by American scientists, it became imperative to appropriate money in sufficient quantity to develop the actual weapons swiftly. But this required public passage of legislation by Congress, and any appropriation of a sufficient sum to carry out the totally secret program could only take place in the altogether public arena where elected practitioners of congressional debate pride themselves in exposing the intimate details of every new public program.

The vexing question of how to get the money without exposing the vastly important secret weapon was brought personally to Speaker Rayburn by top defense officials.

Rayburn faced the problem candidly in the only way he knew. He very frankly and openly, in the briefest possible terms, verbally assured the House that the nature of that appropriation could not be divulged, nor lengthily discussed, without destroying its value, but that he personally had looked into the matter and that, in his honest belief, passage of the legislation could hasten the favorable military end of the war.

With no more comment from any source, the Speaker called for a vote, and the legislation passed unanimously!

There is no parallel to this, I am assured, in the history of the Congress. From this I think it may be concluded that, of all our distinguished presiding officers, Sam Rayburn deserves recognition as the one who, in the face of dire necessity, could confidently call upon the unanimous personal trust and honor of the entire American Congress.

• • •

There's one other aspect of Mr. Sam's unique leadership style that I must mention here. It is the Speaker's personal manner in asking for a vote from an individual member on a controversial topic.

This personal episode which impressed me lastingly occurred in 1957 and involved the very first civil rights bill that had passed the US Senate since Reconstruction days, almost a full century earlier.

Previously to this occasion, some senator or group of senators always had filibustered any such bill to an untimely death if it appeared anywhere near likely to pass. On this rare occasion, thanks to the efforts of Senate Majority Leader Lyndon Johnson, the bill had passed the Senate. For once, the House vote would be determinate.

This bill was under debate on the House floor when Speaker Rayburn sent a page to ask me to come to the front of the chamber and visit with him briefly.

"Jim," he said, "I think you want to vote for this bill. I know you are receiving a lot of angry letters threatening you with all manner of retribution if you do. But I believe you're a big enough man to overcome all of that. And I know you'll be proud in future years that you did."

He was right on all counts. I did want to vote for the bill, and did so. I was indeed receiving a load of angry "hate mail" with only faintly veiled threats. But somewhat surprisingly, I suffered no lasting political harm, and I am, as Rayburn prophesied, proud that I did.

And, as you most surely can discern, I'm happy that I lived and served in an era that let me have the friendship and example of Speaker Sam Rayburn.

John Kennedy campaign rally, Burnett Park, Fort Worth, Texas, September 13, 1960. At bottom, from left to right, Senator Ralph Yarborough, Speaker of the House Sam Rayburn, Dee J. Kelly. At top, from left to right, Senator Lyndon B. Johnson, Senator John F. Kennedy, and Representative Jim Wright. *Courtesy Dee J. Kelly.*

2

# Memories of Sam Rayburn

## *A Conversation with Dee J. Kelly led by former Congressman Pete Geren*

*Before the interview began, Dee J. Kelly addressed the guest of honor, Speaker Jim Wright:*

Jim, I think you know how much, more than I do, that Mr. Rayburn admired and respected you as a person and a member of Congress. I recall when you first ran for Congress, you ran against a man named Wingate Lucas, who was the incumbent congressman from Fort Worth. He was supported by Amon Carter—one of the most powerful men in the country and especially in Fort Worth. Mr. Rayburn was very pleased when you defeated Mr. Lucas, because he knew that you would be better for Fort Worth, and how right he was. Mr. Rayburn was right again in his judgment about people who would be successful in Congress. Jim Wright literally got out of his hospital bed to be here to honor Mr. Rayburn today. Thanks for being here, Jim. Neither Mr. Rayburn nor the City of Fort Worth ever had a better friend than Jim Wright.

Pete Geren (PG): Dee, you met Mr. Rayburn when you were still in high school. How did you meet him? What was he like as a person? I think you campaigned with him—talk about that.

DJK: It was during my junior year in high school that I first met Sam Rayburn, who was then Speaker of the US House of Representatives.

Mr. Rayburn was already a legendary figure in the Congress and by far the most famous man ever to come out of Fannin County.

The first time I ever met Mr. Rayburn was at his home on Highway 80. I wrote a column for the high school newspaper and got to interview Mr. Rayburn. I recall distinctly asking his advice for young people. He replied that he had always found that hard work was the distinguishing characteristic of successful members of Congress, and that applied to the young as well as to others.

Later, I campaigned with Mr. Rayburn in the rural areas of the Fourth District. We would drive to small towns for political rallies in a pickup truck, where Mr. Rayburn would address the crowd from the platform of the pickup bed. One of the first things I noticed about Mr. Rayburn was his uncanny ability to remember names. He could remember three generations back.

I remember on one occasion seeing Carl Albert at one of Mr. Rayburn's campaign speeches. He was from McAlester, Oklahoma, and running for Congress. The Speaker told me later that he thought Carl Albert had a bright future in the House, and so he did, when he later became Speaker of the House.

PG: You grew up in Bonham, Texas, Sam Rayburn's home when he served in Congress and was Speaker of the House. Talk about Sam Rayburn and his relationship with his hometown and his constituents. What did people think about him?

DJK: Despite his enormous power, Mr. Rayburn was a humble man who never lost his roots. I rode from Denison, Texas, to Washington, DC, on the train with him. He slept better than I did.

I recall a hot Saturday afternoon in July, when George C. Marshall came to Mr. Rayburn's office. As chief of staff, Marshall organized the largest military expansion in US history. At that time, General Marshall was secretary of state under President Truman. While General Marshall was waiting to see the Speaker, the Speaker got word that a couple of friends from Ector, Texas, near Bonham, were sitting in a car parked next to the Capitol. They were embarrassed to come to his office because they were not dressed properly. Mr. Rayburn slipped out the back door of his office, went downstairs, and visited with this couple briefly before returning to his office to keep his appointment with General Marshall.

PG: You worked for Mr. Rayburn in Washington. How did you get that job? What were your responsibilities? Please tell us about his office. What was the size of his staff? How did he handle constituents?

DJK: After graduating from TCU in 1950, I was able to get a clerk's job with Mr. Rayburn while I attended law school at George Washington University.

I worked at the Speaker's congressional office, which was located on the south part of the Capitol. My work in the Speaker's office was routine clerical work, typing letters to constituents and running errands for the Speaker. Back in those days, the House always recessed no later than August 1. The Speaker's staff was small and consisted of seven people. Pete, you probably know more about how many people work in the Speaker's office now than when Mr. Rayburn was there.

Mr. Rayburn had a habit of going to his parliamentary office on the north end of the Capitol after the House session concluded and then, generally, to return to his congressional office later to check his messages. This was usually at or about 5:30 p.m. All of the staff would be gone, except me. I would wait deliberately in the hopes that Mr. Rayburn would come around, which sometimes made me late for law school. But when he came around at 6:00 one evening and I was still there, he raised my salary the next day!

PG: The "Board of Education" was held in a private room in the Capitol. I understand a lot of the business of the Congress took place in that room—very different from today's Congress. Please tell us about the Board of Education.

DJK: Mr. Rayburn had a room on the first floor of the Capitol, which was known as the "Board of Education." He hated that name. The Board of Education was a room where Mr. Rayburn retired at the end of the day. You may remember he was a bachelor. It was considered a great honor for either a House or Senate member to be invited for a drink in this room. It was in this room that many important legislative decisions were made, particularly when Senator Johnson became majority leader of the Senate.

I somehow got a key to the Board of Education and while the House was in recess, and Mr. Rayburn was in Bonham, I would go there to study. I remember the room had various kinds of refreshments, but mostly "Pinch Bottle" Scotch. Subsequently, when Mr. Rayburn discovered that I had a key to the room, he quickly acquired it and that was the last of my days in the Board of Education.

PG: Vice President Truman joined Mr. Rayburn in that room sometimes, did he not? Share memories you have of President Truman's visit to the Board of Education.

DJK: Harry Truman was there when he first received word of President Roosevelt's death. He was in the Board of Education room when Mr. Rayburn took a call from Stephen Early, the White House press secretary.

President Truman and Mr. Rayburn were great friends. The only picture on President Truman's desk at the Truman Library, besides his wife, was that of Mr. Rayburn.

I recall watching television when President Truman made his first address to the joint session after President Roosevelt's death. He was very nervous and started speaking before the Speaker had a chance to introduce him. I distinctly remember hearing the Speaker say to President Truman, "Harry, Harry, please let me present you."

When President Truman left office, he refused to accept Board appointments, and he would not accept fees for speaking engagements. When he left the White House, he had no job. He wrote Mr. Rayburn and asked him to try to get him a presidential pension. Mr. Rayburn finally succeeded in doing so at $25,000 a year—the first presidential pension.

PG: President Truman visited Bonham during the 1948 presidential campaign. Please talk about his visit.

DJK: President Truman came to Bonham in 1948 in his campaign for reelection. He arrived on his presidential train, which he had used throughout his campaign. The Speaker had a reception for him at his home and I remember walking through the line and shaking hands with him. It was the first time I ever saw a president of the United States. He was very tanned, had glistening silver hair, and thick glasses that he always wore.

PG: Today our Congress is very partisan. Mr. Rayburn's era was a different time. Mr. Rayburn's relationship with Joe Martin, Republican Speaker of the House, from 1947–1949 illustrates what a different world it was.

DJK: Joe Martin from Massachusetts was leader of the Republican Party in the House. He became Speaker in 1947. It was the first time in twenty years the Democrats had lost control of the House.

He and Mr. Rayburn were good friends. While they were poles apart politically, Mr. Rayburn would never hear a harsh word against Mr. Martin. In fact, when the Democrats regained the House, Mr. Rayburn let Mr. Martin keep the Speaker's office at the south end of the Capitol and Mr. Rayburn continued to occupy the minority leader's office.

Mr. Rayburn and Joe Martin served as leaders of their respective parties. Between them, there was bipartisan agreement on foreign affairs and national defense matters.

FDR called Mr. Rayburn during the development of the atomic bomb. It was a matter of utmost secrecy, because the Germans were trying to develop the bomb as well. Mr. Rayburn was able to procure the necessary funds without any reference to the weapon itself. I suspect that Joe Martin may have been involved in this matter as well. The funds were provided and timely.

In August of 1941, months before the Japanese attacked Pearl Harbor, Mr. Rayburn supported the draft bill. It passed by one vote.

PG: Do you have any memory of the Cadillac car that the Democrats gave Mr. Rayburn in 1948?

DJK: In 1949, after the Democrats had regained control of the House, after losing it to the Republicans in 1947, the House Democrats gave Mr. Rayburn a black Cadillac. Mr. Rayburn made the mistake of asking me to drive it to Bonham. He stressed to me that I was to take my time and take care of his new car. I drove from eighteen to twenty-four hours straight, driving at night and through fog in the mountains, and somehow managed to make it to Bonham without damaging the car. However, I had the good judgment to wait three days before calling Mr. Rayburn to tell him that I had arrived. If he actually found out how little time I had taken in driving the car, it probably would have been the end of my Washington employment.

PG: LBJ referred to Mr. Rayburn as a father figure to him and often talked about his love for Rayburn. What kind of relationship did they have?

DJK: Mr. Rayburn and Senator Johnson were close personal and political friends. I got acquainted with almost all of Senator Johnson's staff.

Senator Johnson would come to see Mr. Rayburn fairly frequently. Occasionally when Senator Johnson was visiting, President Truman would happen to call the Speaker. Senator Johnson always recused himself when the president called.

When Senator Johnson became the majority leader of the Senate, he and the Speaker ran both Houses of Congress. They would speak daily about the schedule for each chamber.

PG: While you were working with the Speaker, did you have a chance to meet members of the Texas delegation to Congress?

DJK: I met a number of prominent people while I worked for the Speaker. The Texas delegation to the House was extremely powerful. In addition to the Speaker, the delegation included then-senator Lyndon Johnson, Congressman Lloyd Bentsen, and Jim Wright, who were among Mr. Rayburn's favorites. In the case of then-congressman Bentsen, Mr. Rayburn was particularly fond of his wife B. A., a former Conover model.

Some of the distinguished Texans visiting Mr. Rayburn were Sid W. Richardson, Perry Bass, and John Connally of Fort Worth. Mr. Richardson, of course, was a famous Texas wildcatter and his nephew Perry Bass became a legendary figure himself. John Connally acted as their counsel in those days. He later became governor of Texas, secretary of the navy under President Kennedy, and secretary of the Treasury under President Nixon.

PG: What other memories of your working for the Speaker stand out in your memory?

DJK: It was an exciting time in Washington when General Douglas MacArthur returned to Washington after being fired by President Truman during the Korean War. He was invited to address a joint session of Congress. Another of Mr. Rayburn's aides and I came to the Speaker's Room, which was the official office of the Speaker of the House, to await General MacArthur's entry. When General MacArthur entered the room, the other aide and I said: "Good morning, General." He ignored both of us and went directly to a large mirror behind the Speaker's chair. Then he removed his famous hat and placed it on a receptacle and attended to his hair, what little he had. I remember he had a little more hair than you do today, Pete. He was later accompanied to the House Chamber by a group of members, both Republican and Democrat, and as he left I slipped into the rear of the House Chamber and stood within a few feet of him as he addressed the joint session. This was the famous speech where he concluded by saying, "Old soldiers never die; they just fade away." It was a very dramatic speech and I never heard the House Chamber so silent. When he concluded to a standing ovation, I rushed over to the parliamentarian's office again to greet the General when he returned to the Speaker's room. I remember saying: "Congratulations, General." He went right past me, looked at himself in the mirror, picked up his historic hat, and departed.

I recall another occasion when Mr. Rayburn and I went to Greenville, Texas, where he was scheduled to address a political rally. He kept a Chevrolet at the Rayburn home, and for some reason, he decided to drive himself that evening. By that time, Mr. Rayburn had been Speaker for almost ten years and he was chauffeured everywhere he went. Consequently, it was rare for him to drive. I recall well when we got to Greenville, we did not know where we were going and decided to make a left turn. Unfortunately, that turn was onto a one-way street. I said, "Mr. Speaker, I think we are on a one-way street." His head began to turn red and he said, "By God, I think you are right," and made an immediate right turn. We then crossed the main thoroughfare of the city of Greenville. Unfortunately, as we began to cross the intersection, there was a huge truck barreling right down on us very fast. I leaned over to the Speaker and said, "I think that truck's going to hit us." He speeded up just in time for us to avoid the premature loss of this great statesman. Needless to say, I drove back to Bonham that evening.

Another occasion I recall was being single virtually all the time that I worked for the Speaker. I remember an occasion when Mrs. Lyndon Johnson asked me and Warren Woodward, a staff member for Senator Johnson who was also single at the time, to take out two young ladies. I took out her niece and Woody took out a girl from San Antonio.

Mr. Rayburn heard about us taking these girls out, so he decided to help us. He made available his limousine with his driver, George Donovan. He asked what we planned to do. We told him we were going to dinner at the Shoreham Hotel and to the Shubert Theater. He thought that was a good idea, so he decided he was going to pay for the evening, and he reached in his wallet and handed me a twenty-dollar bill. Mr. Rayburn was a frugal man, but the twenty-dollar bill didn't go very far, even in those days, especially for four people.

Later that same evening at the theater, we saw several celebrities, including the secretary of state and his wife—Mr. and Mrs. Dean Acheson. In fact, they were about two rows in front of us. After the show was over, we went back to the front of the theater and stood around watching all the important people go by. After a while, we noticed that the secretary of state had not left and his limousine was parked behind the Speaker's. Finally, Mr. Donovan, the driver, found us and in a sense of great exasperation told us to get in the car quickly because the Secretary of State could not go home until the Speaker's limousine left first. So, because we did not understand the political priorities of governmental limousines, the Secretary and Mrs. Acheson got home late that evening.

PG: You were with Mr. Rayburn at the 1960 Democratic Convention. I understand that Mr. Rayburn and then former President Truman tried to help LBJ get the nomination over Kennedy. Tell us about that effort—the Kennedy and LBJ debate.

DJK: I remember attending the 1960 Democratic National Convention in Los Angeles as an aide to Mr. Rayburn. President Truman, Mr. Rayburn, and John Connally were all supporting Senator Johnson to be the nominee for president.

Sid Richardson died in 1959. At the time, Mr. Connally was working with Perry R. Bass and had been named as an independent executor under Mr. Sid Richardson's will. For a time, he served as an officer of the Richardson Foundation, where Pete currently serves today as director.

President Truman was not in attendance, but he and Mr. Rayburn and John Connally spoke frequently by telephone during the convention. They were doing everything in their power to assist Senator Johnson in getting the nomination for President, but he was an underdog to Senator Kennedy. Mr. Rayburn, President Truman, and John Connally conceived the idea of challenging Senator Kennedy to a debate before the Texas and Massachusetts delegations. They all thought that Senator Kennedy would probably not accept because he was so far ahead in committed delegates. To their surprise, he did accept, and the debate between them was one of the most exciting political events I ever witnessed. Jake Pickle was the doorkeeper at the debate, and he tried to keep me out. However, I did get in.

Senator Johnson performed extremely well, explaining how he had to attend to business as Senate Majority Leader while then-senator Kennedy was out campaigning. Senator Kennedy's response was to brag on the majority leader, hoping that he would continue in that position and told the audience in all good humor that he did not have to worry about the Senate as long as Senator Johnson was there running it. It was a marvelous performance by both candidates, and all done in the very best of good humor.

There was considerable speculation about who would be vice president if Senator Kennedy got the nomination. I remember eating lunch with Speaker Rayburn and Edward R. Murrow, the famous correspondent and TV personality. Mr. Murrow asked Mr. Rayburn if Lyndon Johnson would accept the vice presidency. Mr. Rayburn made it clear in no uncertain terms that he was opposed to it and did not think that Senator Johnson should do it under any circumstances.

PG: After JFK got the nomination, did Mr. Rayburn help LBJ get the vice president position?

DJK: When it became apparent that Senator Kennedy was going to get the nomination, I left Los Angeles and returned to Fort Worth. No sooner had I arrived than it was announced that Senator Lyndon Johnson had accepted the vice presidency. I called Mr. Rayburn in Los Angeles and asked him what had happened, and he replied, "Lyndon did the only thing he could do." Mr. Rayburn was always a team player.

Later, President and Mrs. Kennedy charmed Mr. Rayburn. I recall a picture of Mr. Rayburn fishing, and it had a note attached to it from Mrs. Jacqueline Kennedy, saying "We know who the big fish is, don't we?" There was another note on it from President Kennedy saying, "Yes, we do." One of President Kennedy's strengths was his self-depreciation, which was witnessed in the debate before the Massachusetts and Texas delegations.

PG: After the election, I understand Mr. Rayburn helped Connally get a job with JFK. Tell us about that.

DJK: Mr. Richardson and Mr. Bass frequently invited Mr. Rayburn to San Jose Island, and John Connally would be present. They would shoot quail and wild turkeys on the island. There were also deer and other game on the island.

When Mr. Rayburn got ready to leave the island, Mr. Bass always made sure that he received all the game that was killed during the visit. Mr. Rayburn would then go back to Bonham and split it with his brothers and sisters. I recall he had ten brothers and sisters.

Mr. Rayburn was not the best shot in the world, but on one occasion John Connally thought he had made a shot and exclaimed: "Great shot, Mr. Speaker!" The Speaker said: "John, I didn't fire my gun." There was no question that Mr. Rayburn was fond of John Connally.

I recall being in Mr. Rayburn's home in Bonham one afternoon when then-president-elect Kennedy called the Speaker to consult him regarding people for his Cabinet. Mr. Rayburn described John Connally as one of the ablest young men in the state. John Connally always believed that was the major reason President Kennedy later named him as secretary of the navy.

PG: Mr. Rayburn died in 1961, while still serving as Speaker of the House. There are famous photographs showing Presidents Kennedy,

Johnson, Eisenhower, and Truman in attendance at his funeral. Share your memories about his passing—when you learned of his death and memories from the day of the funeral.

DJK: Sam Rayburn died on November 16, 1961, of cancer. I would often go to see the Speaker at his home in Bonham. He would complain about his back and I do not think he ever did know what was truly wrong with him. I remember the funeral being attended by President Kennedy and Vice President Johnson, along with former Presidents Truman and Eisenhower.

The minister who conducted Mr. Rayburn's funeral was a Baptist preacher from the small town of Ector, Texas. Having this gentleman to do the eulogy again reflects Mr. Rayburn's never losing contact with his roots.

I attended the internment service at Willow Wild Cemetery in Bonham where I saw President Eisenhower trying to find his car after the service was over. I helped him locate it. There were no Secret Service agents attending former presidents back in those days.

PG: Mr. Kelly, do you have an opinion as to why Mr. Rayburn was able to make history by staying in the important office of Speaker for seventeen years?

DJK: Mr. Rayburn was a born leader. He was a small-town rural conservative, who also labored successfully to achieve social reform. He could be both conservative and progressive. But what was really important was that he was a man of great sympathy and feeling for the needs and rights of other people.

President Roosevelt relied on Mr. Rayburn when the House passed the Social Security Act. As you have heard earlier today, while as chairman of the Interstate Commerce Committee, he authored some historic legislation that remain in effect today. There was the Rural Electrification Act and another involving farm-to-market roads reflecting his interest in those who lived in rural areas.

PG: Dee, isn't there a sculpture plaza in Bonham displaying selections from speeches by Mr. Rayburn?

DJK: Yes, sir. There is a more than life-size statue of Mr. Rayburn, thanks to the generosity of the Sid Richardson Foundation and the Burnett Foundation. The plaza also includes passages from speeches made during Mr. Rayburn's career. My favorite quotes are these:

> When a voter asks me a question, I treat him the same way as I do my colleagues who have honored me . . . in our national Capitol for so long. I tell him the truth the first time. I never have to remember my answer then, for it will always be the same.
>
> I have always dreamed of a country where lawmakers had no other purpose than to write just laws that shall in the years to come be of service to citizens yet unborn.

*Dee J. Kelly ended the session by again addressing Speaker Wright:*

Jim, if the Speaker could be here today, he would say; "Well done, Jim Wright. You made it a better place for us to live in Fort Worth and throughout the country. You served your country well and nothing could be said more of any man." God bless and keep you, Jim.

YOUR VOTE AND INFLUENCE APPRECIATED
SAM RAYBURN
of Fannin County
CANDIDATE FOR REELECTION
CONGRESS
FOURTH CONGRESSIONAL DISTRICT
Composed of
Collin, Fannin, Grayson, Hunt, Kaufman,
and Rockwall Counties
Subject to action Democratic Primary, July
(Over)

Portrait of Representative Sam Rayburn, ca. 1914. *Harrison and Ewing, Photographers, Collection of the Library of Congress.*

# 3

# Sam Rayburn and the Fourth Congressional District

Anthony Champagne

## *Introduction*

When Sam Rayburn is discussed, it is usually in the context of his role as the longest-serving Speaker in American history. During that time, he served as the link that held together the northern and southern wings of the Democratic Party in the House of Representatives. Or Sam Rayburn is mentioned as the powerful chair of the Committee on Interstate and Foreign Commerce, where he served as the workhorse of the New Deal, responsible for such major legislation as the Truth in Securities Act, establishment of the Securities and Exchange Commission and the Federal Communications Commission, the Public Utility Holding Company Act, the Emergency Railroad Transportation Act, and the Rural Electrification Act.

Rayburn was elected to the US House of Representatives in 1912 after serving three terms in the Texas House of Representatives, the last as its Speaker. In 1931 he became chair of the Committee on Interstate and Foreign Commerce and in 1937 became majority leader. He became Speaker in 1940, minority leader in 1947, Speaker again in 1949, minority leader in 1953, and Speaker in 1955 until his death in 1961.

However, one does not serve in the top leadership of the US House of Representatives nor amass an extraordinary legislative record without being elected from a congressional district. When Sam Rayburn died, he was the longest-serving member in the history of the House of Representatives. Today, he is still the sixth longest-serving member. This paper will explore the district that sent Sam Rayburn to Congress for forty-nine years and will examine how Sam Rayburn was able to be elected as its representative through twenty-five elections.

## *The District*

Sam Rayburn's initial foray into congressional politics cannot be understood without understanding the political dynamics of North Texas politics early in the twentieth century. Joseph Weldon Bailey, from Gainesville, Texas, was Sam Rayburn's early political mentor. He was the most controversial political figure in Texas politics. He had been elected to Congress from the Fifth Congressional District, which included twelve counties in 1890, reduced to six counties in 1893. He served in the House until 1901, when he went to the Senate, where he served until 1913. His old House seat was occupied by Choice Randell from Sherman, Texas. Randell was a member of the Ways and Means Committee and served in Congress from 1901 to 1913. He was elected from the Fifth District in 1900, but then was elected from the Fourth District after some redistricting in 1902. The new Fourth District included Collin, Fannin, Grayson, Hunt, and Rains Counties. Randell was facing reapportionment in 1912 and had come out as an anti-Joe Bailey candidate for the US Senate, most overtly by proposing anti-graft resolutions to prevent members of Congress from receiving gifts or fees from anyone with business before Congress. Those resolutions were clearly aimed at Joseph Weldon Bailey, who had gotten rich during the time that he was in the Senate representing those with government business. Randell sought a Senate seat in 1912. In 1911 Rayburn was elected Speaker of the Texas House as a Bailey man to protect Bailey from further investigations—Bailey had already been subject to two Texas legislative investigations due to charges of corruption.[1] As Speaker, Rayburn was in a prime position to draw a congressional district that would be favorable to his candidacy. At this point, Rayburn's major political threat was from Lamar County, where state senator B. B. Sturgeon posed a significant hurdle to Rayburn's first step toward election: the Democratic primary. A victory there was tantamount to election. That threat was handled by drawing Lamar County out of the district.[2] The Fourth District was not changed from the old Randell district in 1902. Randell lost his bid for the US Senate to Morris Sheppard and was to remain a political threat to Rayburn for a number of years—his son Andrew Randell ran against Rayburn in the 1916 Democratic primary, and Choice ran against Rayburn in 1930 and in 1932.[3]

Even without Lamar County's B. B. Sturgeon, initial election to Congress was not easy for Rayburn. He had seven opponents in the 1912 primary, and he only received 23.4 percent of the vote. That was enough, however. A majority was not then required for victory, only a plurality, and Rayburn received the highest number of votes.[4]

The Fourth Congressional District was a largely rural district populated by small farmers and small town businesspersons and professionals. Cotton was the main crop and other crops in the district were wheat, hay, oats, and sorghum. Much of the land was rolling prairie with rich, black soil. Even in the early days of the twentieth century, much of this land was "cottoned out"—eroded by one-crop agriculture and poor farming practices. Although rainfall in the district averages just under forty inches a year, that number is misleading since summers are hot and dry, baking the soil and making dryland farming difficult. When it does rain, the thick black clay turns to mud, which makes mobility difficult. In 1960, the largest town in Rayburn's district was Sherman. In 1960, the year prior to Rayburn's death, its population was only 24,988. There were only four other towns in the district with populations greater than ten thousand: Denison in Grayson County, Greenville in Hunt County, Terrell in Kaufman County, and McKinney in Collin County. Fannin, Rains, and Rockwall Counties, three of the counties in the district, had no town with a population as large as ten thousand. Little industry existed in the district, and only in Denison was organized labor strong due to the presence of the Katy Railroad locomotive repair shops. This population of the district was overwhelmingly white, and there were few people of Spanish origin. Only about 14 percent of the population was African American. During Rayburn's congressional career there was little in-migration, and the Fourth District remained agricultural with cotton as the main crop.[5]

Rayburn was only redistricted once during his congressional career. After the 1930 census, it was necessary to change the Fourth Congressional District. It had lost population since Rayburn first went to Congress even though Texas had gained almost two million people. In contrast, the Fifth Congressional District, which was to the south of the Fourth, had grown from 197,449 in 1910 to 387,385 in 1930. Rayburn was pleased with the redistricting: he received two new counties,

Rockwall and Kaufman. He wrote of Rockwall County, "Its people, its industries and its land are very similar, if not identical to other counties of the District." He thought the same of Kaufman County of which he wrote, "I do not know of a county in the State that I would rather have in the district that I represent than Kaufman County, as I feel that the people in that county are fine people and will fit in with the other counties in the district."[6]

Rayburn was not threatened by reapportionment again until the 1950s, when his battle with Governor Allan Shivers erupted over Shivers's disloyalty to the Democratic Party. Shivers and his supporters, it was claimed, intended to defeat Rayburn because they perceived him as too liberal and were opposed to his Democratic party loyalty. The Shivers forces considered redistricting the Fourth District by moving it south into Dallas County. Without a doubt, Rayburn did not want to represent Dallas County. He had been opposed for years by the leading Dallas newspaper, the *Dallas News*. And Dallas was much more conservative than his rural Texas enclave. In 1954, as an example, Dallas elected an ultra-conservative Republican, Bruce Alger, to Congress, and kept him there for a decade. Rayburn could neither abide Alger personally nor could he stand the conservative policies that Alger espoused.[7] Years later, when Shivers was asked if he would have really reapportioned Rayburn, he denied it, claiming that Rayburn was too important to Texas to push him out of office through redistricting.[8] Several of those closest to Rayburn believed Rayburn contacted a number of people influential in Texas politics and made it clear that if his district was not protected, he could no longer be counted upon to protect Texas interests such as the oil depletion allowance.[9]

Still, it was hard to overlook the small size of Rayburn's district in the 1950s. Rayburn's advantage in the legislature was that State Senator A. M. Aikin, a long-time Texas legislative power, was chairman of the subcommittee considering reapportionment. Aikin's home county was Lamar County, which in the 1934 redistricting Aikin's senior law partner had sought to put in Rayburn's district when Rayburn instead received Kaufman and Rockwall Counties. He was also a friend of Rayburn's and told other senators, "If any of you can go up there and beat Sam Rayburn, have at it, but I am not going to sit here and see him legislated out if I can help it."[10] Rayburn met with Senator Aikin and Senator Aubrey B. Crawford, two of the three senators on the redistricting subcommittee. He told them, "Don't put Cooke County on me and don't put Highland Park [a very wealthy Dallas County city] on me. That silk stocking district doesn't want a Democrat in it." Aikin asked, "Mr. Speaker, you have told us things not to do—what are you telling us really to do?" Rayburn urged that no changes be made in current districts and that instead the new congressional districts should be at-large. Rayburn also communicated with Texas Attorney General John Ben Shepperd. He asked Shepperd, "Why couldn't it be worked out so that the Dallas District be left like it is and mine like it is?" Though Rayburn claimed he wanted Lamar County, he explained that he would not want to take it from his friend, Wright Patman. If he had to take either Denton County or Cooke County, he explained to Shepperd that he would prefer Denton County since he thought Cooke County was nearly Republican.[11] There was no redistricting, and Texas got a congressman at-large.[12] The Supreme Court decided *Wesberry v. Sanders* in 1964,[13] which required reapportionment of seats in the US House of Representatives based upon population, but this was after Rayburn's death. During his lifetime, he had the advantage of a compact, low-population, rural farming district that was ideal for his policies and his political style.

## *The Rayburn Policies*

One of Sam Rayburn's mentors was John Nance Garner, who said, "Every time one of those Yankees gets a ham, I am going to do my best to get a hog."[14] Much like Garner, Rayburn realized that an important underpinning of a long career in the House of Representatives was being an effective member. That meant that the member had to show the voters in the district that benefits flowed to the district due to the effectiveness of the district's congressman. Sam Rayburn was responsible for a number of projects that directly benefited his district. Probably the two most important were farm to market roads and rural electrification. Rayburn was fond of saying, "I want my people out of the mud and I want my people out of the dark."[15] Wright Patman, in an interview with Joe Frantz, recalled how Rayburn provided federal funding for farm-to-market roads. Patman recalled,

> I was in Mr. Rayburn's office when he was Speaker one Saturday after-

noon, and Bill Robinson of Utah, who was chairman of the Committee on Roads and Highways, came in—John Holton [Rayburn's administrative assistant] brought him in . . . and said that Mr. Robinson wanted to talk to Mr. Rayburn about the bill that they had just reported out. A big highway bill. Mr. Rayburn said, "Bill, what's in that proposal for a farm-to-market road?" He said, "Well, we don't have anything written in there specifically, but the agencies in distributing and allocating the money can take that into consideration and make it anything that they feel like is justified." He went ahead and made a little stump speech for that, and the only way they could do it. Mr. Rayburn said, "Well, I feel very strongly about that. I want you to take that bill back and bring out at least 30 percent of that money to go to farm-to-market roads." Bill Robinson said, "Well, I'll do my best on it." He went back and in a few days he reported to Mr. Rayburn that he had an agreement out of them; that if we bring the bill up, the committee would support an amendment to make it 30 percent.[16]

Rayburn knew how important farm-to-market roads were to his district, where wet weather turned the black land into a bog that was impassable. In speeches in the district, he would speak of the value of hard-surfaced roads.

I've been out on a farm and was so lonely that I was just hoping somebody would pass so I could see a horse or a wagon go by. When you are bogged down out there and can't go anywhere, the farmers can't get their children to school, and they can't get their produce to market, they can't get to a doctor if they are sick."[17]

Rural electrification was probably the legislation for which Rayburn was most proud. Speaking about the failure of private utility companies to electrify rural America, Rayburn recalled:

[I]n my county in the early 1930s there was not a mile of rural electrification in that great rich county of 45,000 square miles. Finally there was one mile built. That farm on which I live is a mile from the city limits. We finally got rural electrification out to that farm, and it was the only mile in the county until after rural electrification came about. The rates were such that we could not operate an electric stove on that farm. We could not as farmers pay the bill.[18]

The Rural Electrification Act changed the way electricity was provided to rural areas, so that instead of private utilities, farmers would create nonprofit cooperatives. The co-ops would borrow money from the Rural Electrification Administration, build their electric lines, and repay the loan through electricity sales to farmers. Farmers could also borrow money to wire their farms and to purchase electric appliances. The program proved a rousing success, in spite of the utility companies' claims that rural electrification could not work. Rayburn said, "They said it would never work. But they had never seen a mother and sister over a washtub as I had; they had never seen them heating irons in a fireplace; they had never stuck their hands in dirty coal-oil lamps."[19]

The Denison Dam and Lake Texoma was another Rayburn project—the largest public works project in the district and of great importance to the northern part of his district along the Red River. The river was prone to floods that caused havoc in Texas, Oklahoma, Arkansas, and Louisiana. A dam at Denison would control half the waters of the river and protect roughly 1.6 million acres of land from floods. Additionally, hydroelectric power would be generated, which would insure a power supply for the area. The construction of the dam would also supply jobs to an area greatly in need of employment opportunities. The project proceeded in fits and starts. In 1935 FDR promised Rayburn that funds would be in the 1936 budget for a detailed survey for the dam, but it was not.[20] Rayburn had publicized the promised survey and it had caused great embarrassment to him, along with considerable difficulties in the 1936 Democratic primary. Not long before the primary, FDR visited Denison during a whistle-stop tour of the Southwest and announced approval of funds to begin the Denison Dam survey. Five thousand people came to Denison to greet the President when his campaign train pulled into town. FDR, who was very popular in the district in 1936, made it clear to Rayburn's constituents that Rayburn had an important role in Washington. Within months, the Corps of Engineers opened an office in the Citizens National Bank Building in Denison. They worked in the area for a while and then left, returning in 1938 to draw specific plans for the dam. On June 29, 1939, the *Denison Herald* ran a special edition of the paper that carried the news that Congress had appropriated $5 million to begin constructing the dam. Hundreds of people in Denison held an unplanned parade to celebrate the development. On August 22, 1939, Denison held a formal event to honor

Rayburn for his role in getting the dam. Struggles over the dam construction remained, however. There were engineering problems such as protecting the Cumberland oil field at Madill, Oklahoma, from being flooded, and there were highways and bridges and railroad tracks that had to be moved and rebuilt. Three thousand graves had to be moved from forty-nine cemeteries. There was political and legal opposition to overcome as well. Oklahoma governor Leon Phillips opposed the dam and argued that 100,000 acres of land in Oklahoma would be destroyed and removed from tax rolls, that Oklahoma might not be compensated for damage to roads, and that property owners were not adequately compensated. Phillips argued that the dam would change forty miles of boundary between Oklahoma and Texas. He added that the project was unconstitutional. The arguments made it to the US Supreme Court twice before the legal issues were settled.[21] Phillips's opposition led the Oklahoma legislature to instruct its congressional delegation to oppose the project. At the time, Rayburn was majority leader, and one author claims that Rayburn suggested to the Oklahoma congressional delegation that out of respect for the state's desire to protect its farmland, Oklahoma would get no federal funds for any water project. That led the Oklahoma legislature to withdraw its instruction.[22]

One of the problems of a massive public works project like the Denison Dam and Lake Texoma was that landowners would have to sell their land to the government for the dam and lake. That could create opposition to Rayburn from landowners in the district who might feel mistreated by the exercise of eminent domain. Anticipating that problem, Rayburn attempted to minimize the harm to landowners by insuring that two of his key allies in the district, Lee Simmons and Samuel Fenner Leslie, would handle land valuations and acquisitions in the government's purchases of property.[23] Lee Simmons was appointed to assess the value of property, and Leslie was appointed special assistant to the US Attorney in the Land Division of the Attorney General's Office. He worked closely with Lucius Clay in handling land acquisitions. As Leslie described his job,

> Sam Rayburn was solely responsible for my being appointed assistant United States attorney. I was in his district, and there was talk that he would lose votes if he took land away from the people and I tried to treat them all right. He carried Grayson as well as he did

> Fannin County and he didn't lose any votes in Grayson County for that purpose.[24]

Additionally, when the dam and lake were constructed, there was much low-cost land available in the area for those whose land was taken.[25] Much of the land being taken was flood land as well, so its owners had no special affection for it.

In 1944, as Rayburn faced one of the toughest political challenges of his career, opponent G. C. Morris accused Rayburn of being ineffective as a national leader and ineffective in gaining federal projects for the district. In reply, just days before the election, Rayburn dedicated the $54,000,000 Denison Dam.[26]

Another major water project he spearheaded in the district was Lake Lavon. While not a power source like the Denison Dam, Lake Lavon was important for water supply, for soil conservation, and for flood control. Rayburn was also largely responsible for a number of smaller lakes in the district. In Fannin County alone, these lakes included Lake Fannin, Bonham State Park Lake, Coffee Mill Lake, and Davy Crockett Lake.[27]

Related to lake construction was Rayburn's interest in soil conservation programs, which were important to the district because of erosion problems caused by poor agricultural practices and over-dependence on cotton farming.[28] There were numerous temporary projects that Rayburn brought to the district as well, such as Civilian Conservation Corps camps during the Depression. During WWII there was a POW camp located in Princeton in Collin County and another in Terrell in Kaufman County. The POWs worked on neighboring farms, which helped to relieve the farm labor shortage during the war.[29]

Rayburn's success in bringing such projects to the district as rural electrification and the Denison Dam explains the support for him by those interested in the economic development of the district. And, of course, Rayburn was mindful of the political implications of these projects. He was able, for example, to get a veterans' hospital and domiciliary located in Bonham, which provided 350 jobs to a community where wages tended to be considerably less than the government pay scale. Most of the domiciliary jobs were civil service, but on the day that the personnel officer for the domiciliary moved to Bonham, Rayburn met with him and discussed the importance of hiring local people. For the next three years, the personnel officer had regular meetings with Rayburn during which Rayburn informed him of constituents who were interested in positions, and the personnel officer informed Rayburn of vacancies and civil service examination times and dates. Amazingly, even as Rayburn presided over the House as Speaker in the midst of the Korean War, he took interest in the appointment of nurses, groundkeepers, cooks, and butchers in the domiciliary.[30]

Rayburn also secured a veterans' hospital in McKinney that had 1,500 beds and was designed to serve the North Texas area as a major center for the care of those wounded in WWII. He was instrumental in getting four army air corps bases located in the district during WWII. One was near Sherman in Grayson County, one was in Bonham in Fannin County, one in Greenville in Hunt County, and one in Terrell in Kaufman County. The largest was Perrin Field in Sherman, which graduated 5,500 pilots from its basic flight school. Rayburn also unsuccessfully lobbied for Perrin Field to be the location of the new US Air Force Academy. Although Sherman and Perrin Field did make it to the finalist category, Colorado Springs was chosen as the Academy's location.[31]

There were numerous smaller projects in the district for which Rayburn was responsible, as well. For example, on one occasion the Bonham Chamber of Commerce was involved in a downtown beautification project, and several members of the Chamber's beautification committee gathered at Rayburn's home to talk to him about it. Rayburn had just returned from a trip to South Carolina, where he had spoken to five hundred people in a National Guard armory. This led to Rayburn suggesting that Bonham needed an armory because there was no place in Bonham where five hundred people could gather. The problem was that Bonham did not have a full National Guard unit, and was not therefore eligible for a new armory. About a month later, Robert West of Honey Grove and Aubrey McAlester of Bonham had a meeting in Dallas with General Carl Phinney, head of the National Guard in Texas, so they could talk about prospects for a Bonham armory. Before they could broach the idea, General Phinney stated that Bonham would be getting a new armory. It was clear to McAlester that Rayburn had explained to Phinney that he wanted a new armory for Bonham, even if it meant changing the regulations.[32]

It seemed clear that the Fourth Congressional District had a representative who could get things done and who could bring projects to the district that could lead to improvements in the lives of people who lived there. In addition to the characteristics of the district and Rayburn's effectiveness, however, there was a third factor that explained his political success. That was the Rayburn style.

## *The Rayburn Style*

In the district, Rayburn presented the image of a lifelong farmer. When in Bonham he appeared relaxed and informal. He was at ease in identifying with farmers and establishing relationships with them. Rayburn had grown up on a farm and had known poverty in his youth. He understood the difficulties of farm life. Many of the people in his district shared his farming background, which allowed him to convey the impression that he was one of them. He conveyed the image of a farmer in government who was trying to alleviate some of the drudgery of farm life. One of his friends well described the image he projected.

> Many times I have heard him tell the story of his little country schooling and his mother and father. I think this is what gave him such great ties to his people. As a country kid myself, and going to a three teacher school, gosh, I could relate to that. So could everybody in his district. We all felt like he was one of us.[33]

Rayburn wore tailor-made suits in Washington and had a chauffeur-driven limousine. In the district, he often would wear khaki pants and a white shirt. Instead of riding in the limousine at home he was often seen in his pickup truck, in his sister's Plymouth, or being driven by others. Generally, the limousine stayed in the garage.[34]

Rayburn took great pride in being a man of his word. He never gave promises lightly and projected an image both of unpretentiousness and of personal honesty. In a 1922 speech, for example, Rayburn said, "I have been unable to save much money in my life. I have been in politics, and an honest man in politics does not get rich. I have been kept broke by making campaigns in this district every two years. But every dollar that I have saved has been invested in a little farm."[35] In a 1932 election flyer, there was also stress on Rayburn's personal honesty. "We submit that Sam Rayburn owns no stocks or bonds, but that his savings are in a farm in Fannin County; that he was reared on a farm and that therefore he has the interests of the farmer at heart...."[36] In his approach to voters, stress on personal character was important. One of his supporters pointed out:

> He would go around and meet people all over the district. He wouldn't promise all sorts of things he knew he probably couldn't deliver on. He tried to tell them something about himself, what kind of man he was. And then, in effect, he said to them: "If you think I am the kind of man you can feel comfortable with having as your representative in Washington, then I would like your vote. Otherwise, then you should vote for somebody else. I can't sit here now and tell you how I am going to vote on all these issues that are going to come up in the next two years, but I will tell you this. I will vote on each one of them only after a study of the pros and cons and I'll vote to the best of my judgment and conscience.[37]

The small district with little in-migration meant families lived on farms and in the district's small towns for generations. Rayburn had an uncanny ability to remember names, and in dealing with constituents, he was often able to develop a personal connection with them through knowledge of their family members. If Rayburn could not remember a person's name or family connection, he had community leaders or hired local staff who could whisper the relevant name or connection in Rayburn's ear.[38] This personal touch, his appeal to common farming ties, reminders of his role in rural electrification and bringing farm-to-market roads—all had staying power in Rayburn's election campaigns. Rayburn's friends claimed with little exaggeration that he had only one speech, which they called "the four-cent cotton speech." In the speech, Rayburn would talk of the poor economic conditions during the Hoover administration and then talk about how Democratic administrations had improved the life of farmers. At its core was that with Republicans, there were hard times, and with Democrats, there were good times:

> I can remember four and one half cent cotton. I sold one thousand bushels of oats out here one year for ninety dollars. If I had it now I could get one thousand dollars for it. We sold our cotton at twenty-two and one half a bale. Now we can get a hundred and fifty or more. Cot-

ton seed was burned in those days. They are very valuable now because we do not have too much oil of any kind. Cattle, hogs, and oil were selling at a price that it gave nobody a buying power.[39]

But in the district there was one issue where he could not praise the national Democratic Party, but instead had to speak like a Dixiecrat. That issue, of course, was civil rights. Rayburn was a rural southerner and supported segregation, so when President Truman called for a strong civil rights program in 1948, Rayburn knew he could not support it. If he did, he could not have survived politically. In the 1948 Democratic primary, he was faced with a tough challenge that focused on his close ties with Truman and Truman's civil rights advocacy. By 1948, Rayburn may have become uncomfortable with his anti-civil rights stance, and he seems to have begun to moderate his thinking somewhat. For example, he urged that Texas abolish the poll tax in 1949.[40] In the 1948 primary campaign, however, he sounded like a typical southern politician:

> In my announcements in the papers of the district it was stated that I was opposed to the whole civil-rights program. . . . That is and has been my position. . . . I voted against everything that looked like an attack on our segregation laws. . . . I voted against the antilynching bill in the 67th Congress under Republican administration; I voted against it in the 75th Congress under Democratic administration, and I voted against it in the 76th Congress under a Democratic administration.[41]

Civil rights was probably the one issue that could have led to Rayburn's defeat in the district, had he supported Truman on civil rights.

Rayburn's style was intensely personal. Being accessible to constituents was a fundamental rule for Rayburn. When he once called Rockwall County Judge Ralph Hall and a secretary asked who was calling, he berated Hall, telling him that a "servant of the people" should not care who was calling him since he should take calls from everyone.[42] If constituents came to his office in Washington, Rayburn wanted to see them. Sometimes he would lend them his chauffer and Speaker's limousine for a tour of Washington.[43] Close friends might be invited to meetings in the Board of Education, which met in Rayburn's hideaway office in the Capitol every legislative day for drinks and political conversation.[44] Staff was small. The combination of the Speaker's staff and the congressional office staff never amounted to more than seven persons at any point in time. For most of Rayburn's career, the staff was entirely in Washington, although a few would return to the district with him. There was one part-time district office on the square in Bonham, which was primarily used to handle mail when Rayburn was at home. Later the Sam Rayburn Library sometimes functioned as a district office, where Rayburn would meet visitors and the director of the library fielded phone calls for the Speaker. For the most part, however, Rayburn's home on the outskirts of Bonham functioned as the district office and general contact point for Rayburn, his constituents, and visiting dignitaries.[45] For much of Rayburn's career congressional recesses were quite lengthy, and Rayburn would always return to Bonham. He had a desk in his large upstairs bedroom, but he would meet visitors downstairs in a day room behind the living room and adjoining the kitchen. When Rayburn was home, a constituent could make an appointment to see Rayburn or could simply show up at the house. H. G. Dulaney, who was on Rayburn's staff and then served as director of the Sam Rayburn Library, said that one of his jobs was to manage all the visitors who wanted to see Rayburn so that those with and without appointments could see him without too long a wait. Visits with constituents would usually be brief : they would explain their problem, Rayburn would tell them that he would see what he could do, and then after all the visitors were finished, appropriate phone calls would be made or letters written.[46]

His political organization consisted of community leaders from every part of the district. These leaders represented a wide variety of occupations, from farmers and ranchers to small-town bankers and lawyers. One leader ran a furniture store; another was a gasoline wholesaler; some were newspaper publishers; one was a pharmacist. The key was that these leaders were trusted by Rayburn and were his eyes and ears on developments in their communities. The leaders were expected to keep Rayburn informed, to campaign for Rayburn, and to make small campaign contributions. Some of the leaders would give campaign speeches for Rayburn on local radio, but most would host events for Rayburn and garner support for him among other local community elites. Although some of Rayburn's opponents and potential opponents were offered large sums by wealthy anti-Rayburn oilmen and others from outside the district, Rayburn and his organization ran all his campaigns on very modest campaign funding. His personal style and the friends-and-neighbors political organization he had in every community in the district did not require large funds to run a campaign and win an election.[47]

## *Conclusion*

How did Sam Rayburn get elected in 1912 and continue to serve in the House through WWI, the Roaring Twenties, the Great Depression, WWII, the Korean War, the Eisenhower years, and the New Frontier—until his death in 1961? How was he able to be a national Democrat from a conservative southern state and district? After all, his mentor Joe Bailey had failed in national leadership and had ultimately become a political reactionary. John Nance Garner found that by the late 1930s he could not function as a New Dealer, and he returned to his conservative Texas roots. The answer for Rayburn lies in the three legs that supported his long-standing political career: (1) He had a small, stable, homogenous district throughout his career that was largely unhindered by reapportionment problems or by in-migration; (2) He had a record of effectiveness that provided substantial benefits to his largely rural, small-farmer and small-town political base; and (3) He had an intensely personal political style that established a bond between him and his constituents, as well as a political organization that established a bond between him and community elites who also generated support for him among his constituents.

Sam Rayburn, Majority Leader of the House, holds an informal press conference on the steps of the Capitol, 10/19/38. *Harrison and Ewing, Photographers, Collection of the Library of Congress.*

4

# Sam Rayburn and Rural Electrification

*Common Sense for the Common Good*

D. Clayton Brown

It is appropriate for the Jim Wright Symposium of 2015 to celebrate the seventy-fifth anniversary of Sam Rayburn becoming Speaker of the House of Representatives. Rayburn was a highly respected member of the Texas delegation from his first term in 1913 until his death in 1961. He served as Speaker of the House longer than any person in the history of Congress. At the peak of his Speakership in the 1950s, Rayburn was often referred to as the "second most powerful man in America," second only to the president. There is more to Rayburn, however, than his longevity, because he is identified with some of the major legislative reforms of the twentieth-century Congress, especially during the New Deal years of the 1930s. He was the driving force behind the creation of the Securities and Exchange Commission, the Public Utility Holding Company Act, and the Rural Electrification Act. His name was identified with other reforms, but this chapter will explore his role in the creation of the Rural Electrification Administration (REA). An examination of his part in the REA provides an opportunity to observe his belief, summarized in one his "Rayburnisms," that "if you have common sense, you have all the sense there is."

What is rural electrification? It began with Thomas Edison and his invention of the light bulb in 1879. Edison and others quickly realized the advantage of his invention, and in 1883 the first electric generation station, known as central station service, opened on Pearl Street in New York City. A new industry, the electrical industry, grew fast and extended electrical service to cities and towns across America, so that by World War I the use of electricity in homes was common in urban areas. Rural areas were not served, however, meaning that people living on farms, ranches, and in small towns and villages did not have electrical service. They continued to have a preindustrial lifestyle based in the nineteenth century, as they still pumped water from wells and carried it by bucket into their homes; they continued to rely on the use of the outdoor privy; and they had to use springs or crude ice boxes to cool food. In the northern states, farmers would build small enclosures and fill them with ice cut from local ponds to refrigerate food. The lack of running water and electric refrigeration was responsible for the poorer health conditions and higher disease and parasite rates in rural areas—conditions such as hookworm, pellagra, enteritis, impetigo, and a higher rate of infant mortality.

Without electricity, farmers could not use small electric tools, which meant they had to rely on hand labor and animal power. Such labor-intensive operations kept farms small, accounting for the small scale of dairy and poultry farming. Rural schools could be dark and gloomy on cloudy days, and without radios, people in rural areas were insulated culturally. By the end of World War I a cultural and economic gap appeared between urban and rural residents. Rayburn was well aware of these conditions since he grew up on a small and remote cotton farm in northeast Texas, having none of the modern conveniences found in cities and towns.

Why did the utility companies refuse to serve the rural areas? Privately owned electric companies had to practice economies of scale, that is, they depended on large volume or high numbers of customers to regain their large investment. Electric companies needed to serve areas with a high population density—cities and towns. Power companies could not gain enough revenue from farms and rural homes since they were widely scattered. In 1930, for example, the national average for the number of farms per square mile was three. Three customers per mile could not use enough electricity or generate enough revenue to justify the cost of constructing power lines through the countryside. In 1930 the US average rate of farms with service was 10 percent. California had the highest rate with 60 percent, owing to the widespread use of irrigation to pump water, and the New England states averaged 40 percent. States in the South had the lowest average, about 5 percent, and some of the cotton growing areas had 3 percent or less. Even middle-class farmers in the South and Midwest went without electricity. If farmers were willing to pay the cost of constructing power lines to their homes and forfeit ownership of the lines to the companies, they could get service. Prior to World War II the cost of building lines reached $800-$1,000 per mile. Rates per kilowatt-hour were also high, and farm families could not afford such cost. Consequently they lived without electric lights, radio, running water, and other convenient uses of electricity. Urban residents regarded farm life as preindustrial, primitive, and backward. They often ridiculed and mocked their brethren in the countryside and called them "hillbillies," "country bumpkins," and "hayseeds." For lack of electricity in their homes, farm families had second-class status.

Where was Rayburn during those years? He was born in a log cabin in 1882 in Roane County, Tennessee. At the age of five his family moved to northeast Texas, onto a small cotton farm near Bonham, Texas. The soil was rich and farmers could grow long-staple cotton that brought a premium price. Life on cotton farms was lonely and remote, and Rayburn used to say that as a child he wished someone would come down the road. The Rayburns had a strong work ethic, a high sense of fair play, honesty, and integrity. They epitomized the cotton culture of endurance in the face of hardship. Rayburn served a short time in the Texas legislature before he was elected to Congress in 1912. He won every subsequent election in the Fourth Congressional District for the rest of his life. In 1916 he built his home from a Sears Roebuck kit on the western outskirts of Bonham, with acreage for crops, hay, and pasture. The house was substantially modified and rebuilt over the years that followed. He was able to have electricity extended to his house because he lived on a main road only a short distance from the county seat of Bonham.

During the 1920s the availability and cost of electricity became a national issue. It centered on the question of Muscle Shoals, the hydroelectric dam built by the federal government during World War I. When construction finished in 1920, there arose the question of possession or ownership of the dam, which generated large volumes of electricity at low cost. But the government was not in the business of generating and selling electricity to the public. Such practice amounted to government intervention and federal competition with private enterprise. Henry

Ford offered to buy the hydro dam and sell the electricity at low cost. Ford, like many people, believed the cheap energy would attract heavy industries into the area; he also anticipated selling the energy to the farmers in the Tennessee River Valley. In other words, Ford offered a plan that would diversify the economy in the Valley and simultaneously offer rural residents the opportunity to obtain electrical service. Ford's offer gained much attention and popularity, but he had opponents. Led by Nebraska Senator George Norris, opponents of the plan thought the Muscle Shoals hydro dam should remain in government ownership on the grounds that taxpayers had paid for it, and the energy there could be devoted to public use at cut-rate costs. In other words, the small towns and farmers would enjoy electrical service at low cost, during a period when many felt that utility companies charged exorbitant rates per kilowatt-hour. Norris managed to keep the Muscle Shoals plant in government ownership, but the issue festered throughout the 1920s and early 1930s. The Tennessee River Valley was not the only area where public power had importance, but it was the focus of the issue.

During those years, 1912 to 1931, Rayburn worked quietly and effectively; he served on the House Committee on Interstate and Foreign Commerce. In 1931 he became chair of the committee, which put him into a powerful position once the New Deal administration of President Franklin D. Roosevelt started in 1933. For one thing, Rayburn's party, the Democrats, controlled both houses of Congress and the White House. In the 1930s his committee oversaw legislation that led to the creation of the Securities and Exchange Commission, the Public Utility Holding Company Act, and the bill that created the Rural Electrification Administration in 1936.

The real crusader for rural electrification was not Rayburn or Norris; it was Morris L. Cooke from Philadelphia. A mechanical engineer in private practice, Cooke had become interested in the question of rural electrification soon after World War I ended. He recognized that utility companies had legitimate reservations over serving farmers and sought to find a way for them to overcome the financial and technical barriers that blocked the extension of electrical service into the countryside. Cooke had a more balanced view than Norris's one-sidedness toward the issue of public power. Rayburn, too, would demonstrate a view similar to Cooke's. The latter served as adviser to Roosevelt when he was governor of New York, and became President Roosevelt's confidant on public power issues. Cooke had campaigned in the executive branch to get a program started on behalf of rural electrification, and in 1935 when Roosevelt received a large appropriation from Congress to fight unemployment, he created the Rural Electrification Administration (REA) by executive order and earmarked a large portion of the funds to begin a program to extend rural service. He named Cooke as the administrator of the new REA.

Cooke went to the utility companies in hopes of working out a plan for cooperative action with the REA. Cooke's vision for rural electrification demanded "area coverage," which meant that all rural residents in each area of service would have to be furnished with electricity. Utility companies, on the other hand, generally had extended service only to the prosperous or large farms and ignored the small and ordinary farmers. It was this point of contention that prevented Cooke from making any progress during 1935. He entertained the idea of the REA helping farmers organize and operate electric cooperatives, but still made little progress. Cooke became worried about losing the program, and Senator Norris, along with other public power advocates, feared that unless new action was taken, the effort to expand rural electrification was in danger of a serious setback. It was their apprehension that eventually prompted the creation of the REA by Congress in 1936.

Cooke had moved closer to the use of cooperatives because of the experience of the Alcorn Rural Electric Cooperative established in Corinth, Mississippi, by the TVA. In 1934 officers of the TVA decided to experiment with a rural electric cooperative, to determine if farmer-owned and managed cooperatives were a feasible means of distributing electricity. Operating an electrical grid with retail service requires technical and engineering knowledge, but it also necessitates management knowledge in organization and finances. Could farmers and rural leaders handle such an operation, even with oversight from a federal agency? The Alcorn Cooperative, organized at a meeting around a wood stove in the back of a hardware store on a cold winter day, quickly proved to be a great success. That success encouraged Cooke to move forward toward a program using cooperatives, but he feared that the slow rate of progress by the REA as a temporary agency would jeopardize his objective. This background was vital to the congressional authorization of the REA in 1936.

Cooke engaged in an exchange of letters with Roosevelt and Norris about putting the REA on a permanent statutory footing, both of whom supported his proposal. They also agreed that Rayburn, Chair of the House Committee on Interstate and Foreign Commerce, should lead the fight in the House even though other champions of the cause were available. Congressman John Rankin of Mississippi was a strong advocate of rural improvements, but Rankin, though an avid supporter of public power, did not have the calm and careful poise of Sam Rayburn. Rankin, too, was a strong segregationist. Rayburn had a more balanced position on the question of public power, believing that shunning the private utility companies was not wise. "I think there is a field for both of them," he would say.[1] By the same token, he was not a handmaiden of the private interests, as demonstrated in the House battle over the Public Utility Holding Company Act. In the House, where support for the utility companies was strong, Cooke needed Rayburn. In view of Rayburn's background on a Texas cotton farm and his reputation for effectively managing heated bills through the House, Cooke recruited him to join in the fight for the REA.

Norris introduced a bill in the Senate. He encountered little opposition, although he had to trim the funding for which he originally asked, and he agreed with a proposal to set the amortization period for loans to REA cooperatives to twenty-five years. With these changes, Norris's measure passed easily and it was shuffled over to Rayburn's committee.

In March 1936 the Committee on Interstate and Foreign Commerce commenced hearings on the REA bill. There was strong opposition to the Senate bill among some committee members, who felt it was unjust to exclude privately owned utilities from participating in the program. Cooke testified for three days before the committee, trying to get the members to accept the Norris version that excluded the electric companies. Cooke did not think the companies would want to participate and saw cooperatives as the means to forwarding electrification into the nation's countryside. Committee members disagreed, responding that some rural areas would be too poor to organize and operate a cooperative.

Norris's bill had frozen the rate of interest on the REA loans to cooperatives at 3 percent. Cooke wanted the Committee to accept this provision, but again he ran into stiff opposition. Norris had set the 3 percent rate because that was the current rate that the federal government paid on money that it borrowed. If interest rates climbed, the

REA would become a subsidized program, a possibility that irritated some committee members. Rankin stood with Norris on the measure, but he was outnumbered. Spokespersons for the utility companies requested that private interests be eligible, but otherwise industry representatives put up a mild fight because they had just been defeated in the battle over the Public Utility Holding Company Act and did not want to go through another fight. Rayburn indicated that he saw utility participation and a flexible rate of interest as acceptable. Thus, the committee passed the bill with two critical amendments to the Senate version: electric companies would be eligible to borrow REA funds, and the rate of interest for loans to cooperatives, or companies, would be flexible. Even with the amendments, the committee approved by a margin of one vote. With the amended version, Rayburn took the bill to the House.

Rayburn had to defend the bill from conservatives who wanted to kill the measure completely and public power advocates who wanted to exclude utility companies entirely.

Conservatives warned that trying to establish rural electric cooperatives was unrealistic, that the technical, engineering, and financial requirements for such undertakings were beyond the capabilities of farmers. This same fear had admittedly worried Cooke in the earlier years; the Alcorn cooperative had put Cooke, Norris, and public power advocates in general at ease on the subject. Rayburn, too, trusted the ability of local rural interests to organize and operate electric cooperatives, but he answered that utility companies should be eligible to use REA funds and develop those areas where farmers could not get the job done. He further reminded them that rural residents so desperately wanted electricity in their homes that they would not let their cooperative become insolvent and fail. Best to leave the bill unchanged, he urged, and provide the farmers with opportunity to obtain service either through cooperatives or privately owned companies.

To the measure's opponents from the left—the public power enthusiasts led by Rankin, who had a sense of indignation—there should be no inclusion of private interests in any program launched on behalf of rural electrification. Rankin and his followers had experienced years of frustration with utility companies, which had shown no inclination to serve rural families. Rayburn understood their frustration and the resentment of farmers toward utility companies for not serving them, but he also knew that to get the bill passed, compromise was necessary. For this reason, Rayburn stood by the measure as reported out of his committee, repeating that a balanced approach made the best sense. It would just be common sense, he would often say, not to be one-sided on issues as sweeping and comprehensive as a national rural electrification program.

Rayburn saw danger coming from Rankin—he feared that Rankin would offer an amendment to exclude private interests and that conservatives would support such a change as a procedural move to kill the bill when it came up for a general vote. The future Speaker moved swiftly and asked for a vote on the bill as it stood without amendments. Seeing that utility companies would be eligible and that the rate of interest would be flexible, Rayburn's colleagues passed the REA bill. It went to the Conference Committee, where, Norris later remarked, "the real battle developed" because the House conferees insisted on keeping the House amendments in the bill.[2]

Norris generally was the only Senate conferee that attended. Rayburn led the House attendees; Rankin and two House members, Carl Mapes of Michigan and George Huddleston of Alabama, accompanied him. The group had several meetings with neither side making concessions, and it appeared that the REA would die in the Conference Committee. It looked worse when Norris announced that future meetings were a waste of time, and that he was going to make rural electrification as a wholly public enterprise an issue in the upcoming 1936 general election. He then stormed out of the room.

Rayburn followed him out. "Now Senator," he said, "don't be discouraged. . . . We will come together because we have made up our minds you are not going to give up." Rayburn sought to soothe Norris. "Just let it rest awhile . . . within a few days we will notify you we are ready to have another meeting."[3] Rankin also tried to soothe the Senator, even while both of them agreed philosophically on the issue. Rankin persuaded Norris to give the matter another few days.

The fundamental question was subsidization. Should rural residents use electricity at a cost subsidized by taxpayers? The utility companies had long insisted that nearly all farms able to pay without subsidy were already served. Concerns by private interests had some legitimacy: Cooke had earlier admitted in the House hearings before Rayburn's

Committee that subsidies might be required for some recipients of REA electricity.

Cooke recognized that the deadlock in the Conference Committee jeopardized the REA. He suggested to Rayburn that the rate of interest on REA loans be no more than the rate paid by the US Treasury on its obligations. Such a provision left room for changes in the rates, but REA would, of course, always match the Treasury rates. Such a measure satisfied Norris that the current rate of REA interest would be 3 percent. Cooke then told Norris that the question of participation by utility companies was academic because they would not agree to provide area coverage. Cooke also conferred with Rayburn and told Roosevelt that the disagreement was "likely to be resolved."[4]

Compromise was in the air when the conferees met again. Rayburn brought up Cooke's suggestion about the rate of interest, and Norris agreed. He further agreed to let utility companies be eligible for REA loans, but only after preference had been given to cooperatives. The House and Senate accepted these revisions, and Congress passed the bill on May 11, 1936. Roosevelt signed the bill a few days later, and the Senate confirmed Cooke as the new REA administrator on May 26.

History has given Norris the title of "father of the TVA," and understandably so. The REA, despite its impact in changing rural life throughout the United States, has never attracted the attention that the TVA did. For that reason Rayburn has not been noticed like Norris for his contribution to rural electrification, but Cooke later recalled that Rayburn and Norris had an equal role in the creation of the new REA.

Congress authorized funding for the revised agency, and REA electric lines began appearing around the United States. By the end of 1941 the number of farms and rural homes with service had reached 30 percent, but that figure included the 10 percent already served by the utility companies in 1936. With American entry into World War II, funding was greatly reduced, and construction moved at a snail's pace. At the close of the war, however, Congress threw money at the REA, sometimes giving the agency more money than it wanted. The REA had become widely popular, and Congress intended to finish the job of extending electrical service throughout America. In 1955, 90 percent of the farms and rural homes in the United States had service, a figure generally deemed to be completion. Work continued for the remaining homes and farms until the task was fully accomplished.

REA's impact was immediate and profound. Farm families nearly always spent money on the following electrical conveniences: wiring for incandescent lighting, a radio, and an electric iron. Running water and indoor bathrooms always came later, owing to the higher cost of installing them. Electrification went a long way in modernizing rural America, and for good reason Rayburn always regarded his role as a favorite accomplishment. On the matter of solvency and financial management of farmer-owned cooperatives, the rate of default on REA loans came to only one percent, an astounding figure that any banker would like to have.

Without Rayburn's common-sense, middle-ground philosophy, the REA bill would probably not have passed. The program would likely have had to wait, perhaps until after World War II, delaying the modernization of rural America for another generation. Norris, Rankin, and public power enthusiasts wanted no part of the private interests, but their view, while popular in some circles, did not represent all points of view. Rayburn did not want to punish utility companies; he wanted to get electric service to farm families as quickly as possible.

How should Rayburn be judged? He was not the crusader for rural electrification. That distinction belonged to Cooke, who had fought the battle for most of his professional life. Norris was the champion of public power in view of his long-time fight on behalf of the TVA. Rayburn was the legislator who prevented polarization and enabled Norris and the crusader Cooke to realize their dream. For good reason Rayburn would say, "If you have common sense, you have all the sense there is."

## *The Southwestern Power Administration*

Rayburn's contribution to rural electrification, in which he again displayed his "common sense" approach, occurred with the creation of the Southwestern Power Administration (SPA) in 1943. The Red River, the boundary between Texas and Oklahoma, had long been known for its flooding and destruction for both states, plus Louisiana. Like many others, this river was seen as a potential source of hydroelectric power if a dam and reservoir were built on it. As early as the 1920s local interests in the area around Denison, Texas, wanted to control flooding, but they also saw an opportunity to generate power to serve farmers in the area. Only about 3 percent of the inhabitants had electrical service. A group organized in the Denison area to get a hydroelectric dam built; a representative of the Denison group told the House Committee on Flood Control in 1930 that the greatest benefit from the structure would be electricity. "You can light up that whole country and turn every barn into a factory by giving farmers the power. . . . we will milk the cows, run the refrigerators, rock the cradles, fry eggs, and bake the cakes with electricity."[5]

Rayburn's Fourth Congressional District included the Denison area, and he understood the need for electricity there. Rayburn took the leadership role in pushing for the dam: he organized the Red River Flood Control Association and arranged for spokespersons to appear before congressional committees. He was responsible for getting the US Army Corps of Engineers to survey and study the area for a dam.

Rayburn had another crusader on behalf of hydroelectric power in the area: Congressman Clyde T. Ellis of Arkansas. Elected to the House of Representatives in 1938, Ellis wanted to erect a similar structure on the Norfork River. Ellis wanted to expand electrical service throughout the northern Arkansas area by getting a dam erected on the Norfork with hydroelectric generators. He visited Rayburn, now House majority leader, and General Julian L. Schley, chief of the Army Corps of Engineers, attended the meeting. Rayburn introduced them and told General Schley that "this boy . . . and I want power put in our dams and mean to get it." Schley pointed out that the utility companies would put up a fight, but Rayburn replied, "We'll take care of that . . . you just get your house in order . . ."[6] The Corps of Engineers drew up plans that included hydro-generators, and Ellis won approval for his dam in 1940. Ellis's fast progress in getting congressional authorization for his dam was unusual for a freshman legislator and it showed how he benefited from his common cause with Rayburn. Ellis resembled Norris in his beliefs about public power: he was no friend of private interests and talked about establishing a "little TVA" in the Southwest. Such talk alarmed the utility companies that saw the talk about rural electrification as a pretext to drive them out of the market in the Southwest.

The utility companies fought back and had a chance, because Congress had not designated any authority or agency to operate the dams once they went into operation. The private power companies in the area wanted to control both structures and hoped they could use this opportunity to obtain control over other hydroelectric dams already approved by Congress. Structures such as these had been placed under the Federal Works Administration (FWA), an agency regarded as sympathetic to private interests, in order to supply defense industries. The Corps of Engineers also was sympathetic to them, and when General Philip B. Fleming proposed putting the Red River and Norfork dams under control of the utility companies, it appeared that Rayburn and Ellis might lose.

The fight over the dams at Denison and Norfork were part of an even larger struggle. A decision had to be made about the final placement of several dams around the United States, and Secretary of the Interior Harold Ickes wanted them placed in his department. Ickes thought only he could keep them out of private hands. Ickes also wanted authority to set rates, an authority that rested with the Federal Power Commission (FPC). Leland Olds, chairman of the FPC, saw Ickes as a threat to his agency, although Olds favored public control of the structures. Olds nonetheless backed Fleming. Such interdepartmental squabbling caused a delay in making the final decision. Rayburn favored Ickes because he thought Interior would be more amenable to Congress, and, of course, Ickes was a public power zealot. Fleming's move, however, caused Rayburn not to wait until the end of the war to take action.

Rayburn had Alvin J. Wirtz of Austin, Texas, prepare a presidential order placing the Denison and Norfork dams in the Department of the Interior, which Rayburn discussed with Roosevelt in July 1943.

After the conference with the president, Rayburn went home to Bonham for a short vacation. From there he wired Roosevelt and stated that he did not want the dams placed in the Federal Works Administration and he asked the president to wait until he had a chance to discuss the matter with him. Then Rayburn wired James F. Byrnes, head of the Office of War Mobilization, known as the "economic czar," and asked Byrnes to take up the matter with the president.[7] A few days later Roosevelt sent a wire to Rayburn, stating that he had just placed the dams at Denison, Norfork, and Pensacola into the Department of the Interior. He also authorized the Secretary of the Interior to set rates. The electricity would first be offered to public entities such as REA cooperatives before utility companies could buy the energy. Ickes then created the Southwestern Power Administration (SPA) to oversee the operation of the dams and named Douglas G. Wright as administrator. Ickes put the SPA headquarters in Tulsa, Oklahoma.

Ickes had wanted the dams, but could not get the president to move on his request. Rayburn, now Speaker of the House, had much prestige in the Democratic Party, and Roosevelt remembered that Rayburn had been instrumental in his nomination by the party in 1932. But the executive order was temporary, so with the Flood Control Act of 1944 the structures were permanently placed into the Department of the Interior.

Wright now faced a dilemma. During the dry months of summer, the Denison dam especially had insufficient water to enable the structure to provide a steady flow of electricity. So Wright arranged a system in which SPA power went to the utility companies in the "wet" months and the companies gave back power during the "dry" months. This system of cooperation owed its origin to Rayburn. As he would say, "We have two schools of thought on the issue, but I think that there is a field for both of them."[8] In view of the weather and geography of the Southwest, for Rayburn cooperation between private and public interests made common sense.

Rayburn's sense of fair play and cooperation was rooted in his background on the Texas black soil that provided high yields of cotton. In that late nineteenth-century environment, his values and views were shaped and molded, fitting into an agrarian lifestyle in which a man's reputation was only as good as he word. Wealth and power did not define men in that time—a man's honesty, his trustworthiness, and his willingness to overcome differences of opinion made the man. Rayburn demonstrated these qualities throughout his life, which caused one news commentator to say upon Rayburn's death in 1961: "He was the salt, soil, and substance of our political system and inheritance. We shall not see his like again in the Speaker's chair, for the old ways, the old image of America are going as the old men go."[9]

Mr. Rayburn's "Little Room Downstairs," US Capitol, known as the "Board of Education" circa 1950s. *Courtesy Office of the Clerk of the US House of Representatives.*

5

# Sam Rayburn and the Texas Congressional Delegation

JAMES W. RIDDLESPERGER JR.

Any examination of Sam Rayburn must begin with his leadership in the nation's Capitol and the driving force he applied to national politics during the era extending from 1937, when he ascended to party leadership in the House, until his death in 1961. He was the dominant force in the House during those years, and through his protégé Lyndon Johnson, often had vicarious leadership responsibilities in the Senate as well. Examination of what made Rayburn tick inevitably goes back to his hometown of Bonham, Texas. It was the culture and politics of small town Texas that framed his understanding of the hopes and aspirations of the American people and that led to his practical, no-nonsense persona.

But if national politics was Rayburn's primary arena, and local politics formed his worldview, his path to political leadership and the context of his political power base were in the state of Texas. In the days before national media turned all issues into national issues, often the most important politics in framing a politician's career was at the state level. Rayburn, like most of the major congressional leaders of his era, got his start in the Texas state legislature, and used that position as a springboard to Congress. His success was facilitated by the relation ships he made in Austin and the mentors he first encountered there. In order to have influence in Washington, he reasoned, one must first take care of one's home state. Texas, then, became the focal point of his power base, the center of his political circle of friends, and the object of his patronage. In a real sense, though he had close relationships with members of Congress across the nation, in both political parties, and over multiple generations, his political family began, and ended, in the Texas delegation.

## *Rayburn as Protégé*

Rayburn learned loyalty to Texas and to Texans in the delegation from his two mentors—Joseph Weldon Bailey and John Nance Garner. Bailey had been the congressman representing Rayburn's district early in Rayburn's life, and his oratorical skill inspired the young native of Bonham to seek a career in politics. Rayburn remembered at about age fifteen riding eleven miles on the back of a mule in the rain to hear Bailey speak. That experience was transformative. Rayburn described Bailey as the "Adonis of a man with a massive brain [who] captured my imagination and became my model."[1]

Early in his political career, Rayburn found himself defending Bailey from allegations of unethical behavior. In 1907, the days before the passage of the Seventeenth Amendment calling for direct election of US Senators by the voters, senators were selected by the state legislatures. And the Texas legislature was examining Bailey's relationship with the Waters-Pierce oil company, a relationship that had transformed Bailey's personal finances from struggling financially to a position of great wealth. Rayburn sided with Bailey in the ethics fight out of loyalty to his mentor.

His early loyalty to Bailey was repaid fully by Bailey's political help to him. In only his third term in the Texas House, Rayburn decided to run for Speaker. Bailey, needing a friend in Austin to prevent future investigations, actively supported Rayburn, encouraging the "Bailey men" in the legislature to "get right" and vote for Rayburn. Rayburn's victory was in part attributable to Bailey's support.

When Bailey left Congress, it created another opportunity for Rayburn. Though Bailey left the US House in 1901 for a Senate seat, and Rayburn wasn't elected to the House until 1912, Bailey was able to throw his support to Rayburn when Rayburn decided to move from the state house to Congress.

If Bailey was Rayburn's first inspiration in politics, it was John

Nance Garner who became his primary tutor in the ways of Congress. When Rayburn came to Washington in 1913, Garner was there to greet him and take him under his wing. Garner used his influence to get an appointment for Rayburn to the powerful Committee on Interstate and Foreign Commerce, the only committee on which Rayburn ever served and his springboard toward leadership in the chamber.

Later, when Rayburn aspired to chamber leadership in the House, it was Vice President John Nance Garner who became his primary sponsor and assured Rayburn's election in a spirited competition.[2] Garner, violating the principle of separation of powers, used his position as former Speaker and as vice president to work tirelessly for Rayburn's selection as majority leader in 1937. His interceding to get the Louisiana delegation to support Rayburn was probably decisive in Rayburn's election. In those days, election as majority leader put a member in position to be elected Speaker, and when Speaker William Bankhead died in September of 1940, Rayburn moved seamlessly into the Speaker's chair.

## *Rayburn as Delegation Leader*

Once Rayburn was in a position of power, he became a guiding force within the Texas delegation. He took responsibility for enhancing the power of the Texas representatives and became, over time, the patriarch of the Texas delegation. As his tenure in leadership developed, he used four strategies to make sure that Texas was prominently represented in Washington: (1) inviting them to the informal session at the end of each legislative day known as the "Board of Education," (2) making strategic committee assignments, (3) presiding over a weekly luncheon where state business could be discussed, and (4) acting as a mentor for a number of key Texans.

## *"Striking a Blow for Liberty"*

A major part of the Rayburn style was the informal session held each day after Congress dismissed. Known as the "Board of Education," though Rayburn rarely used and did not like that term, the meeting at the end of the day was always an opportunity to have a drink with colleagues (which was inevitably called "striking a blow for liberty") and strategizing about ongoing legislative action. Like previous Speakers, and particularly in the tradition of fellow Texan and mentor John Nance Garner, the room on the first floor of the Capitol became a center of social and political activity. An invitation from Rayburn to "come on down" was more of a command for young members of Congress, and he always made sure that there were a number of Texans in the group. Lyndon Johnson was always a regular, as were future Speakers John McCormack and Carl Albert. Harry Truman was a regular as well, and when Franklin Roosevelt died, the phone call from the White House came to Rayburn's little room. Truman's summons to the other end of Pennsylvania Avenue signaled a transition in presidential leadership.[3]

Texans normally included Homer Thornberry and Wright Patman, but others, including Frank Ikard and Jim Wright, were invited occasionally as well.[4] Other than Rayburn, some people were such regulars at the Board of Education that they had a key to the room. Those regulars included Lyndon Johnson, with whom Rayburn had a special relationship[5] and Texas Congressmen Wright Patman and Homer Thornberry. (Young Rayburn aide Dee Kelly had one at least on occasion.) In this manner, Rayburn always made sure that Texas voices were involved in the day-to-day activities of the House.

Rayburn always controlled the agenda of the meeting, and there might be card playing and story telling going on as well. But mostly, it was a chance for what in modern America might be called networking, and Rayburn made sure that young Texans, along with favorite protégés Richard Bolling of Missouri and Hale Boggs of Louisiana, had the opportunity to jumpstart their congressional careers. The cardinal rule, according to D. B. Hardeman and Donald Bacon, was that "anything discussed in the room was strictly graveyard." Even trusted reporters would be invited, so long as they respected the secrecy rule. There's no record that anyone ever violated Rayburn's confidence when it came to the Board of Education.[6]

In addition to inviting members of the Texas delegation down to the end-of-day session, Rayburn would occasionally invite constituents to attend. In so doing, he put a face on the needs of his constituents for legislative leaders to see, at the same time underscoring his commitment to the folks back home.[7] Overall, the tone of the Board of

Education concentrated on power in the House, but Rayburn regularly made sure that the discussion had a distinctly Texas flavor.

## *"Franking Privilege in Washington, Heel Leather at Home"*

Board of Education sessions were one way for Rayburn to get young Texans into the heart of decision-making for the House, but the central organizational feature of the Texas delegation was in the weekly delegation luncheon on Wednesday, where Texans would hash out Texas issues. One week, the luncheon would be an open session, where members could invite family, friends, or constituents to interact with members. But on the alternate week, proceedings were confidential. Jim Wright remembers that on these weeks, "free from prying eyes and ears, each member could say what was on his mind or report arcane intelligence to the group without fear of being quoted outside of the familial confines of the delegation." Such confidence was sacrosanct, and Rayburn tolerated no deviance from the confidentiality norm.

When Bruce Alger was elected to Congress in 1954, he would change the dynamic of the meeting. First, he was a Republican in an otherwise exclusively Democratic group. And second, though there had always been strong conservatives among the Texas delegation, Alger set a new standard for conservatism. These factors would have already set Rayburn on edge, but they were not the cause of Alger's fall from Rayburn's grace. Rather, it was that Alger told the press details of what went on during the private sessions at least twice, and then had the temerity to question Rayburn's motives. Rayburn, said Alger, cared more about his party than his country. After these indiscretions, Rayburn was asked what he thought of Alger. Rayburn's response: "I don't think about him. He is a shit ass."[8] Jim Wright remembers that Alger's sin was not that he was a Republican, but rather that "he had no real regard for the gentleman's rules of the delegation luncheon."[9] And Rayburn followed through on the grudge, asserting that Dallas would not get a needed new federal building as long as Alger remained in office, and diverting funds for that purpose to building the Fritz Lanham building in Fort Worth. Dallas didn't get a new courthouse as long as Rayburn lived, and almost as soon as Earle Cabell defeated Alger in the election of 1964, appropriations loosened and the new courthouse was named in honor of Cabell, a former mayor of the city, but perhaps more importantly, the political slayer of Alger.

The weekly Texas meetings were friendly, and though Rayburn presided over them, there was rarely any arm-twisting during the sessions. Information was shared, but at the end of the day, "every man [was] his own best arbiter of the rectitude of action and his own best judge of what his constituency will swallow."[10]

## *"We pick 'em young, we pick 'em honest, we send them there and we keep them there"*

Rayburn presided over a plan to distribute Texas power broadly across Congress. To do so, he tried to make sure that a Texan sat on all of the major committees in the House. Over time, they accrued seniority on those committees and the power that came with being committee chair. At times, Texans presided over fully half of the major standing committees in the House. Such distribution meant that, according to Jim Wright, "members assumed the responsibility to look out for the interests of the constituents represented by their Texas colleagues even though they might disagree on matters of principle with those individual members. Whenever a Texan had a problem relating to the parochial interests of his constituents, he always had a champion, an intercessor and a friend on whatever committee the bill or the proposition came under. This actually applied without any regard to whether the members agreed with one another on philosophy."[11]

Wright found out about Rayburn's commitment from the outset of his congressional career. Wright had always had an interest in American foreign policy and hoped to secure a seat on the Foreign Affairs Committee, and went to Rayburn to make his wishes known. Rayburn, however, had a different idea. He told Wright that Texas needed a voice on the Public Works Committee, an essential committee for the types of economic development programs that would help the Texas economy grow. Wright, Rayburn thought, might be a perfect person for that job. And as Wright began to build seniority on Public Works, he began to appreciate the wisdom of Rayburn's idea. Moreover, when Wright decided to run for Majority Leader in 1976, his position on Public Works proved a perfect platform from which to launch his campaign, much as Rayburn had benefitted from Garner's wisdom in placing him on Interstate and Foreign Commerce all those years before.

The delegation was often seen as a cornerstone for national politics as well. Rayburn famously worked with Lyndon Johnson to prolong the draft for army service in 1941, even though isolationists who did not want to become entangled in the wars in Europe and Asia wanted to step back from military preparedness for such a war. Johnson and Rayburn met with President Roosevelt in August of that year. When Minority Leader Joe Martin said the Republicans would oppose extension of the draft, Rayburn enlisted Johnson as his chief lieutenant in the House fight. Johnson even made a rare speech on the floor in favor of the bill. Rayburn quickly declared the measure passed when it was announced that 203 members had voted for extension and 202 against.[12] Their work, of course, was proved especially important when the Pearl Harbor attack came in December of that year.

In 1957, Rayburn and now Senate Majority Leader Lyndon Johnson worked to get the first civil rights bill in seventy-five years through Congress. Rayburn pressured the Texas delegation and got the support of most of them. He approached the young Jim Wright and told him that he knew Wright wanted to support the bill but that he, along with others in the delegation, were concerned about its effect on reelection. He counseled Wright that in the future Wright would be proud of the vote, and that he was man enough to withstand the negative publicity a positive vote would generate from some quarters back home. Wright remembers Rayburn's counsel as insightful and even prophetic.[13]

Rayburn gained fame for his adage that "without prefix, without suffix, and without apology, I am a Democrat." For him, that was a part of his being and was not only a definition of his party, but a deep description of his values. In 1952, when many Texas Democratic leaders endorsed Texas-born Republican Dwight Eisenhower for president, Rayburn, though in many ways a fan of Ike, who had been born in Denison, Texas, endorsed and worked diligently for Democrat Adlai Stevenson. For him, the choice was about commitment to his party. Said Rayburn, "Without loyalty, you haven't got a starting place."[14]

Rayburn's daily routine included reading all of the major Texas newspapers in the Speaker's lobby.[15] His passion was for Texas in an age when state and region meant far more emotionally than perhaps they do in the twenty-first century. Rayburn had an abiding love for the small towns of his childhood and for the ideal of a community where "people know it when you are sick and where they care when you die."[16] For him, that place was Bonham, which in many ways represented the best in Texas, and Texas the best in the nation.

## *Rayburn as Mentor*

Rayburn never picked out a single person to focus on as his primary successor in influence in the House. Rather, he mentored members of Congress who he thought had leadership potential without endorsing one as his chosen protégé. At times he was close to a number of younger members of Congress, including Richard Bolling of Missouri (who served Harry Truman's home district in the House), Carl Albert of Oklahoma (whose district abutted the Red River to the north of Rayburn's district), and Hale Boggs of Louisiana, for whom Rayburn had a special affinity.

But Rayburn's most notable protégé was Lyndon Johnson, who cultivated a personal relationship with the bachelor Rayburn. Rayburn had known Johnson's father in the Texas legislature, and became very close to Johnson's wife Lady Bird. Importantly, when LBJ was sworn in to the House in 1937, it was Majority Leader Sam Rayburn who stood by his side.[17] Rayburn would figuratively, and often literally, remain at Johnson's side for the rest of his life. Rayburn and Johnson worked together as national Democrats and New Deal Democrats when other Texans began to dissent from Franklin Roosevelt's agenda. Famously, several key Texans had begun to chafe as the newness of Roosevelt's transformative program began to wear off. John Nance Garner had become skeptical of FDR's domestic agenda and stepped down as Vice President after FDR's second term; Hatton W. Sumners had led congressional opposition to Roosevelt's court packing plan in 1937 and later retired from Congress; and Governor Allan Shivers, a Democrat, had formed a "Texans for Eisenhower" movement in the election of 1952. Through all of these travails within the Democratic Party, Rayburn and LBJ stood shoulder to shoulder as Democratic regulars, loyal to the Texas Democratic Party but solidly within the national coalition as well.

Rarely did a Sunday pass without Rayburn's feet under the Johnson's dinner table. Johnson became something of a surrogate son. How close did they become? When Johnson would see Rayburn in the halls of Congress, he would bend over and give Rayburn a kiss on his bald head.[18] Jim Wright observed that LBJ was the only person in the world who could get away with such familiarity. Rayburn was formal and stern, and nurtured an image of seriousness. Only Johnson could really break that façade at will.

But their relationship was in part a partnership too, and though Rayburn was a man of the House, Johnson wanted to live life at a faster pace and on a bigger stage. They argued frequently, but could never stay angry with one another. Though he was always respectful of Rayburn, Johnson often went his own way in terms of his career, with Rayburn famously complaining that LBJ was "as independent as a hog on ice."[19] In 1939, Rayburn wrote a response to Johnson's birthday wishes, responding to Johnson's statement of great respect and admiration with a reply ending "I am always glad to be of service to you—you are an apt pupil." By the time Johnson had ascended to the majority leader position in the Senate, the student had become a partner, and in the judgment of one journalist "the pupil had outdistanced the master in legislative acumen."[20] It is doubtful Johnson would have completely agreed, but it is clearly the case that they had different time references, and different sets of loyalties from time to time. LBJ was addicted to the most modern technology, and Rayburn preferred the simplicity of rural life. Johnson was among the first people in Washington with a car phone; Rayburn would say "I never get a call so important that it can't wait until I get to my apartment."[21]

One illustration of their struggles came with the 1940 struggle over Franklin Roosevelt and the third term. Both Rayburn and LBJ had been loyal New Dealers, but Rayburn also felt an uncompromising loyalty to his old mentor, Vice President John Nance Garner, while LBJ saw the wisdom in remaining loyal to FDR.

Rayburn's last time to stand shoulder to shoulder with LBJ came when John Kennedy asked that LBJ be his running mate as the vice-presidential candidate in the election of 1960. Rayburn had supported Johnson to be the presidential candidate, and like Johnson, was disappointed when Kennedy got the nod. But he quickly understood Wright Patman's observation that LBJ couldn't turn down the vice-presidential nomination—it would be bad for his career opportunities moving forward, and his candidacy would be a boon to Kennedy's candidacy. So he endorsed Johnson's vice-presidential campaign and worked one last time for the election of a Democratic president.

As he aged, Rayburn lost track of many of the younger members of Congress, and mostly communicated with junior members through committee chairs.[22] But that was not so with the delegation from Texas. The Texas delegation was Rayburn's close family. Rayburn constantly sought out leaders among the Texans in the House and promoted their careers. Though he tolerated wide varieties of opinion even within the delegation, he encouraged them to vote together on issues affecting Texas.

He could also twist the arms of Texans to accomplish goals that he thought served the interests of the United States. Rayburn grew up as a southern segregationist, but he was by southern standards a moderate on the issue. He and Lyndon Johnson worked together to push the 1957 Civil Rights Act through Congress. Rayburn instinctively knew that the time had come for a relaxing of the civil rights lines that had separated southerners from others in the nation. Though he could hardly be called a leader in the civil rights movement, he clearly was the legislative leader of the 1957 act in the House.

Johnson was clearly Rayburn's "favorite son," but when Johnson left the House for the bigger stage of the Senate and to gain a platform for his presidential ambitions, Rayburn had no Texan among those to succeed him in House leadership. Rayburn might have been personally closer to Boggs, Bolling, and Albert than he was to other Texans he might mentor for leadership. And, of course, his relationship with those three fostered them as leaders. Boggs became majority whip before his death in a plane disappearance in Alaska. Bolling used his position on the Rules Committee to seek leadership positions in the House, although he did not succeed—probably because of his abrasive personality. And, of course, Albert succeeded Rayburn as the "southern" representative in House leadership and became Speaker in his own right.

These and others outside the Texas delegation, by age proximity and length of tenure in Washington, may have become close to Rayburn, but there was a younger future Speaker who saw Rayburn as his role model. Jim Wright came to adore Rayburn, whom he saw as more of a father figure than a contemporary in Congress. Rayburn took an immediate liking to his young colleague, as he did to other young Texans such as Jack Brooks. On one occasion, early in Wright's career, Rayburn invited Wright to join him for dinner after the "Board of Education" session. Wright rode with Rayburn to a restaurant in the Speaker's limousine. Rayburn had noticed, to Wright's surprise, that Wright had nursed only one drink in the informal session, and asked Wright why. When Wright said he wanted "to keep his wits about him," Rayburn replied: "You keep that attitude, and there's no limit to how far you can go."[23]

On another occasion early on in his career, Wright showed up to an affair at a Washington hotel in winter without an overcoat. Rayburn noticed that, too. One of Wright's closest aides, Paul Driskell, related a story that Rayburn came up to Wright and said, "Aren't you a member of Congress? And aren't you planning to be in Washington?" Wright replied that yes, he was planning to stay. Rayburn said, "Then you'll need this," and took his overcoat off and gave it to Wright. A day or two later, Wright took it to Rayburn's office to return it. Rayburn looked at him and said: "What is this? Now you're calling me an Indian Giver?" So Wright kept the coat throughout his time in Washington.[24]

Rayburn continued, over the seven years that he and Wright served together, to promote Wright and to train him in the ways of Congress. Their relationship was never as close as Rayburn's had been with Johnson, but it was illustrative of how Rayburn looked after other Texans in the House and taught them the traditions and "folkways" of the chamber. Wright always saw Rayburn as a role model for congressional leadership, and when he came to the Capitol on the day that he was elected majority leader, he wore one of Rayburn's hats. By then, wearing hats had become passé. But Rayburn's influence remained pervasive.

Photo of Congressional Leadership at the White House, from left Vice President John Nance Garner, Senate Majority Leader Alben W. Barkley, Speaker William Bankhead, and House Majority Leader Sam Rayburn, January 9, 1939. *Harrison and Ewing, Photographers, Collection of the Library of Congress.*

# 6

# Rayburn as Leader

## *Strategic Agency and the Textbook Congress*

Douglas B. Harris

## *Introduction*

Sam Rayburn had considerably more influence on the history of the House of Representatives than most of its Speakers and merits mention alongside the most influential and institutionally impactful leaders in House history. To push this point further in a way that would surely provoke controversy among scholars, one could argue that Sam Rayburn is the greatest Speaker of the House in the history of the United States. This is a contention that historians and most political scientists would recognize as valid or at least worthy of serious consideration. An institutional stalwart, Rayburn was Speaker longer than anyone else in House history, serving as Speaker seventeen years in the mid-twentieth century, making him Speaker of what political scientists still call "the textbook Congress." A long-time, faithful Democratic partisan, Rayburn was minority leader when Republicans took control of the Eightieth and Eighty-third Congresses and a key, if cooperative, opposition counterpoint to the president during the divided government of the Eisenhower administration. A policy maker and committee chair before entering the leadership, as Speaker, Rayburn was central to the policy accomplishments of the New Deal, the Fair Deal, and the beginnings of the New Frontier.

The evidence of his historical importance and greatness is manifest. Along with Joseph Cannon and Nicholas Longworth, Rayburn is one of three House Speakers for whom a House Office Building is named.[1] He is also the subject of half a dozen biographies (twice as many as Tip O'Neill, Thomas Brackett Reed, or Joe Cannon, and nearly as many as Henry Clay, although Clay has more than a century head start on Rayburn).

Still, political science theories and studies of legislative leadership have a hard time accommodating Rayburn's greatness and, specifically, his effectiveness as a leader in the House. Inasmuch as most Congress scholars might list Rayburn among the greatest leaders the House has ever known, our theories of legislative leadership would be slow to explain why, and our theoretical treatments of legislative party strength are apt to treat Rayburn as an anomaly—or not to treat him at all. This discrepancy in treatment is likely due not to some unexplained "hero worship" for Rayburn that has exaggerated his effectiveness, but rather to a deficiency in our theories of legislative leadership. Specifically, I argue that it is due to the tendency of political science theories to reserve the greatest laurels for "strong agents" who dominate some aspect of the legislative process or American politics, like Joe Cannon or Newt Gingrich; or for reformers, institution builders, or those who change the institution, like Henry Clay or Thomas Brackett Reed. Fixated as it is on power's blatant exercise or the dramatic nature of institutional change, political science has a harder time recognizing the greatness of the patient leader, like Rayburn, who guided the House and legislation in a steady and stable (today we would say "sustainable") way, mostly preserving the institution's key elements rather than radically changing them.

This chapter focuses on Rayburn's style, effectiveness, and impact as Speaker, seeking at once to make the case for Rayburn's superlative impacts on legislation and the House, and to reconcile that effectiveness with the difficulties it presents for political scientists' understanding of what makes for a great leader. First, I argue that Sam Rayburn was a "strategic agent" as House leader, one who was always searching for supplemental sources of influence and one who was willing and effective in the broad use of that influence. Second, I explore Rayburn's legislative leadership style and how his informal accrual of resources reflects his active pursuit of more leverage and his desire to exert influence—even though the institutional context of the House severely curtailed party leader influence during Rayburn's time. And, third, I consider Rayburn's disposition toward institutional change: rather than seeking to change the House as some legislative leaders and institutional reformers have, Rayburn instead sought to protect the institution that he led, stabilize it, and preserve it throughout his career and—to the extent possible—beyond.

## *Strategic Agency and the Rayburn Speakership*

If popular understandings of congressional politics focus on outsized personalities or on well-managed political images, political science studies of legislative leadership make the opposite mistake. That is, political science theories of leadership shift attention away from individual leaders and their actions and focus instead on the institutional and party contexts within which leaders lead. Most contemporary accounts of legislative leadership posit that leaders are "agents" of their party followers (the "principal") and argue that, as agents, leaders are largely responsive to the demands of the rank-and-file, and their influence is conditioned by the degree of agreement within the party on policy.[2] In most of these formulations agents do the bidding of the principal and generally have few, if any, goals independent of the principal.

The roots of this tendency can be found in scholars' efforts to build upon Joseph Cooper and David W. Brady's seminal article that compared Sam Rayburn's speakership in the mid-twentieth century to that of Joseph Cannon in the early twentieth century. In this article, Cooper and Brady claimed that legislative leadership style and effectiveness are primarily determined not by the "personality" of individual leaders but rather by the institutional context in which they lead. As Cooper and Brady put it, "institutional context rather than personal skill is the primary determinant of leadership power in the House" and "institutional context rather than personal traits primarily determines leadership style in the House."[3] Whereas Cooper and Brady's definition of "institutional context" included such factors as the strength of the party and party system and the formal powers afforded the Speaker by House rules as important elements to which leaders would respond, subsequent scholars have marginalized the role of individual leaders, opting instead to explore how some elements of context, particularly the ideological cohesiveness of the legislative party, predetermines leadership strength and effectiveness.

Following Cooper and Brady (and narrowing the focus of their analysis), most political science studies of legislative leadership borrow from the language of economics and think of leaders in terms of what is called principal-agent theory. Most notable among these theories is David Rohde and John Aldrich's "conditional party government" theory, which says that leaders lead when followers are agreed.[4] That is, when there is agreement within a congressional party on an issue, then the leadership apparatus kicks into gear and leaders are expected to advance the interests of the party and its members. Following this logic, congressional leaders are most influential when followers agree and weakest when there are divisions in the party. In broader historic scope, the theory holds that congressional leaders are strongest in eras when parties are most unified and weakest when parties are divided.

But under this formulation, one wonders if the individuals who occupy these positions matter at all? If legislative leaders (as agents) simply do the bidding of their follower colleagues (the principal), then is it really *leadership* we are talking about? Critics have charged that such theories treat leaders more as automatons or servants of their party rather than as anything that would really merit the term "leader."[5]

In recent years, there has been some correction to this as some scholars have shifted our focus back to leaders themselves and to the strategic contributions to policy, to Congress, and to the legislative process made by a Reed, a Cannon, a Pelosi, an O'Neill, a Wright, or a Rayburn. For example, in his fine book, *The Speaker of the House: A Study of Leadership*, Matthew Green has argued that Speakers have their own goals (including personal and institutional goals) that compete with the broader contextual forces that define a speakership.[6] Given the persuasiveness of Green's treatment of Rayburn's strategic role on several policies,[7] it is clear that Speakers sometimes assert their own goals in making and influencing policy. Ronald Peters and Cindy Simon Rosenthal devote considerable attention to Nancy Pelosi's strategic adaptations to multiple contextual factors to define her own style and expand her effectiveness as Speaker.[8] Another recent work that posited a stronger role for leaders is Randall Strahan's book, *Leading Representatives*. Strahan argued that, under some conditions, leaders are institutional reformers who strategically change the institution in order to lead it. Here leaders like Clay, Reed, and Newt Gingrich are held out as leaders who changed the institution, each leaving an imprint on the Speakership and the House with which subsequent leaders would have to contend.[9]

Still, what are we to make of a leader like Rayburn, whose disposition was to protect the institution, stabilize it, and maintain the status quo? If we are to broaden Strahan's general lesson—that individual leaders are consequential for the history of the House as an institution—then surely that consequence can include the consolidation and preservation of institutions against reform as much as it can include proposing and catalyzing reform itself. This leads to the more general point: scholars are only beginning to understand the myriad impacts that individuals—leaders included—can have in *and on* institutional contexts.

Following these studies, I argue that we should view Rayburn (and other legislative leaders) as *strategic agents* who, regardless of their party or institutional context, seek to be as effective and influential as possible. Their policy commitments matter in the context of the party's collective goals and indeed give articulation to those goals; their sense of what constitutes effective leadership and the skill with which they employ that sense come to define leadership style; and, their dispositions toward institutional stability and change impact the prospects that any significant institutional change will be undertaken. To be sure, *strategic agents* are constrained by institutional context, and their prospects for success are circumscribed by the strength or weakness of the parties they lead. Still, in any context, leaders develop alternative resources that they use to enhance their effectiveness, their autonomy, and their influence.

This focus on Rayburn and other leaders should not be mistaken for an argument against the institutional context theory of leadership.[10] To the contrary, I believe that the impetus for studying individual leaders' contributions can be found in Cooper and Brady's original consideration of leaders in context. Whereas some have argued that Cooper and Brady's model gives the most analytical weight to context, my reading of Cooper and Brady suggests instead that there is great room for individual leaders to define their positions, choose among competing strategies, and to have an impact on legislative outcomes. First, rather than an exclusive focus on intraparty agreement, Cooper and Brady suggest that there are multiple contextual factors that condition leadership strength and style, including House rules, the strength of the party system, and the authority orientations of party members. In such an environment a leader's ability to choose which of these factors should be given most weight is paramount. Moreover, Cooper and Brady were at the forefront of scholarly efforts to introduce leader learning and choice in accounting for institutional change when they describe the emergence of Rayburn's bargaining style. It is difficult to read the following without ascribing some analytic weight to Rayburn's (the leader's) independent skill and judgment:

> The components of this new style emerged gradually in the 1920s and 1930s as power in the House decentralized. It crystallized under Rayburn and was fully applied by him. It represented his experienced and finely tuned sense of what made for effective leadership in a House in which the Speaker lacked the formal powers of a Czar, had to mobilize a majority party fairly evenly balanced between discordant northern and southern elements, confronted a set of committees and committee chairmen with great power and autonomy, and had to deal with individual members who rejected party discipline and prized their independence.[11]

In their account, Rayburn's "finely tuned sense" of how to be effective in the context in which he led was crucial to the development of the bargaining style and thus merits further consideration alongside considerations of context.

To return to my initial argument in this light, Rayburn is arguably the greatest leader in the history of the House because he was remarkably effective (historically effective) in an era when the prospects for party leadership were significantly limited by factors in the institutional context. He had a weak, divided party; keen rivals in the committee system; and few prerogative powers afforded him by House rules. It was in this context that Sam Rayburn had to lead the House as Speaker. He had to serve as a broker of bargains (generally between strong committee chairs), a bridge and coordinator of deals among divergent factions within the majority party, and a practitioner of a highly personalized form of leadership that allowed (even encouraged) members to vote their districts (often against the party) and allowed them to support the committee system (even though organizationally it was the chief rival to the party leadership).

For his part, Rayburn developed a leadership style that was marked by the avoidance of open conflict, by the balancing of northern and southern factions, and by permissiveness.[12] If these are not traditional hallmarks of strong leadership, Rayburn was nevertheless the chief bargainer in the mid-century House. Although he could not be as strong a Speaker as Cannon or Reed, Rayburn sought to maximize his effectiveness within the bargaining role. Perhaps in some ways Rayburn would have hoped for a more favorable context, but as Speaker Carl Albert, one of his many protégés, once said, "You have to plow with the horses you have."[13] That is, if the context suggested the role of a bargainer for Rayburn, as a *strategic agent* he would cultivate the informal resources that would make him a better bargainer.

## *Rayburn as Legislative Leader*

Although Rayburn entered the House post-Cannon but during the height of caucus rule, he became majority leader and Speaker (in 1937 and 1940, respectively) at a time when the revolt against Cannon and progressive reforms outside Congress had significantly diminished the formal strength and internal unity of America's parties. Most directly, the Democratic Party had become deeply divided between its more conservative southern base and its more liberal contingent from the North, the Midwest, and the West. This had considerable impact on the strength and style of party leadership in Congress.

Comparing Rayburn's institutional context to that of Joseph Cannon at the beginning of the twentieth century, Cooper and Brady observed, "Denied the power they possessed over the individual member under Czar rule or caucus rule, party leaders began to function less as the commanders of a stable party majority and more as brokers trying to assemble particular majorities behind particular bills. Denied the power they possessed over the organizational structure under Czar rule or caucus rule, party leaders began to function less as directors of the organizational units and more as bargainers for their support."[14] The sum total of these changes and the ensuing bifurcation in the Democratic Party along regional lines may have decreased party strength in

Congress, but in key respects, they made the tasks and creativity of leadership all the more important. As Cooper and Brady put it simply, "These changes . . . made the task of the majority party leadership more, not less arduous."[15]

If a party could not command member unity on a regular basis, the bases of unity had to be forged, repeatedly and creatively, by a nimble and diligent House leadership capable of building and rebuilding legislative coalitions and willing to ally today with yesterday's opponents, forgiving past disagreements and pragmatically working, both within the party and across the aisle, to move legislation. If all of this is true and these contextual factors worked to undermine strong party leadership, too many scholars have read it to mean that leadership was marginalized and somehow less important. To the contrary, individual leaders and their efforts became *more* important as the functions of brokering deals and building intra-party agreement on legislation became essential. As Cooper and Brady put it, "The result was that by 1940 the personal, political skills of the leadership, rather than its sources of institutional power, had become the critical determinant of the fate of party programs."[16]

Despite the weakness of the party system around him, Sam Rayburn was essential, effective, and personally impactful in the legislative process of the "textbook Congress." Not satisfied with leading as a weak party leader of a weak party era, Rayburn restlessly and *strategically* sought avenues of influence, and he sought to cultivate considerable informal resources to bolster his position within his contextually determined role of bargainer. And it was this array of informal resources that became the hallmarks of the Rayburn leadership style, one that involved the *constant gathering and control of information*, *the accrual of bargaining chips*, and a permissive approach to members who might be unable to support the party leadership on some policy matters.

*Gathering and Controlling Information.* In important respects, the House of Representatives is an information economy and leaders are advantaged to the extent that they can effectively gather, manage, and deploy information resources. Moreover, information was at a premium in the more fluid and generally unpredictable bargaining era of the textbook Congress. In order to effectively lead, a bargaining Speaker or party leader is advantaged to know, first, who might be willing or able to bargain and who will be unwilling or unable to bargain and, second, what inducements they might desire in a bargain.

Rayburn brought to Washington from his district in Bonham, Texas, a penchant for gathering information and a talent for building an elaborate intelligence network.[17] Just as he knew his own district, Rayburn prided himself on knowing most members' districts as well as they knew them. Thus not only did he know when a member had leeway in his or her district to vote with the party and when he or she did not; he also "knew if members were having political problems, if they desperately needed a dam or a federal courthouse in their districts, or if they were having personal or domestic problems."[18] Understanding individual members' reelection imperatives and goals, Rayburn could anticipate needs and cultivate the kinds of sweeteners and inducements that might become useful in luring members to support party-backed legislation.

Rayburn also had an elaborate intelligence system in the House. He famously used his Board of Education, an informal meeting of a small group of members that the Speaker convened at the end of the legislative workday. Noted as a place where prominent House members would drink, share information and stories, and plot together, it was in the Board of Education that Rayburn "learned all the gossip of the House and there he planned much of the House's operations":

> John McCormack reported at these sessions on a host of problems familiar to him as floor leader. [Frank] Ikard kept Rayburn informed on the key Ways and Means Committee, and [Dick] Bolling and [Homer] Thornberry did the same for the Rules Committee. . . . [Lew] Deschler helped in mapping strategy . . . with his intimate knowledge of House rules and precedents. Other influential men of the House were invited to these sessions, particularly when their expert knowledge of specific problems was needed.[19]

Dating back to the Longworth and Garner speakerships, the Board of Education meetings were primarily designed to elicit information from members. Even the tradition of drinking at the Board of Education had its informational purpose: Speaker John Nance Garner once said, "You get a couple of drinks in a young Congressman and then you know what he knows and what he can do. We pay the tuition by supplying the liquor."[20] Interviews with Bolling, Deschler, and [Joseph] Evins led F. Edward Wood Jr. to conclude that the primary advantages of the Board of Education were "the information-gathering and political intelligence advantages."[21]

Rayburn also sought information from nonmembers important to the Capitol or the Washington community. Rayburn gathered information from House elevator operators and key lobbyists. He even had "regular private briefings" from the House physician who "helped Rayburn keep abreast of members' health."[22] Former Congressman Frank Ikard (D-TX) claimed that Rayburn's "intelligence system" included multiple informal contacts: "He had staff people, for example. Also, he wandered around. He knew more people in the House and more staff people than you can imagine. He picked up little bits of information. . . . People knew he was interested in what was going on."[23] Full of resources about the House and its members, Rayburn was active and strategic in his perpetual search for the kinds of information that would make him a more impactful and effective bargainer. As practiced a "reader" of the membership as the House has ever known, Rayburn was ever restless in the search for more and better information. A hallmark of Rayburn's meetings included the Speaker's parting, saying, "Let me know if you hear anything."[24]

Still, to be at the center of a bargaining culture and to be its preeminent bargainer requires not only acquiring information but dominating the information economy. And Rayburn not only sought to gather information but to control it as well. Several aspects of Rayburn's interpersonal and official communication styles facilitated a predominant one-way flow of information toward the Speaker. Most fundamentally, Rayburn was noted both for his taciturnity and for being an extraordinary listener and sounding board, two characteristics that almost guarantee that Rayburn would gather more than his share of information.[25] Moreover, Rayburn often preferred direct one-to-one conversations with members and other people key to the workings of the House. The practice of talking to members directly allowed Rayburn to make personal appeals and, as Dick Bolling put it, to "'compartmentalize' his leadership by dealing with different people on different issues."[26] Thus, many people in Rayburn's orbit would share parts of his knowledge, but only the Speaker (and perhaps his closest lieutenants) would be able to see the whole picture.

A more official extension of this strategy of compartmentalization was the suspension of regular meetings of the House Democratic Caucus. Whereas the House Democratic Caucus had existed since the early days of the American republic and had reached, albeit qualified, policy and organizational importance in the second decade of the twentieth century,[27] the weakening of party throughout the first half of the twentieth century and the bifurcation of the House Democratic Party in the 1940s and 1950s made the Caucus a potentially divisive meeting of the party rather than a force for policy development and intra-party unity. As a result, Democrats suspended regular meetings of the Caucus for most of the "textbook" era, fearing that regular meetings would exacerbate the deep ideological and policy rifts between Southern and Northern Democrats. Whereas the elimination of the Caucus meetings helped Rayburn avoid conflicts among House Democrats, it also yielded Rayburn greater control over the communication between members by keeping them divided—providing Rayburn with a near-monopoly on gauging party sentiment about what the "party agenda" was.[28]

This control over information combined with Rayburn's experience in the House to produce in the Speaker a sense of the House that he thought essential to his leadership. Rayburn once said: "I do know that in the case of the House the Speaker has to be utterly responsive to the waves of sentiment rolling out from its members. If he does not have the *feel* of the House, he is lost and he might as well quit."[29] Rayburn was able to maintain a feel for the House, in part, because he possessed these considerable information resources, thus cornering the market on legislative and political information.

*Accruing Bargaining Chips.* Of course, knowing the House's bargaining environment is only part of being an effective bargainer. Having figured out both who might bargain as well as what these potential bargainers might want, one must then seek to procure the bargaining currency most likely to persuade members.[30] As a strategic agent seeking to maximize his effectiveness in the House, Rayburn sought to *maintain and cultivate a cache of bargaining chips and sweeteners* to smooth over the sometimes difficult process of bargaining.[31]

The centrality, history, and authority of the Speakership made Rayburn key to, if not preeminent in, the legislative process and thus afforded him a number of legislative inducements that could be persuasive in his bargaining with committee chairs and members. Although the power that Joseph Cannon enjoyed in an earlier era to appoint members and chairs of committees was a distant remnant of House rules, Rayburn nevertheless enjoyed some influence in the committee assignment process for Democrats, which for the entirety of Rayburn's Speakership was controlled by the Democratic members of the Ways and Means Committee. When Rayburn stepped in to advocate for younger members to get committee assignments, he made clear their roles, especially if the committee was key to party influence in the chamber. In recounting when Rayburn appointed him to the Rules Committee, Tip O'Neill recalled Rayburn saying, "Now I don't give a rat's ass whether or not you like the legislation. If it's a party issue, your obligation is to get it on the floor. Once it gets there, of course you're on your own and you're free to vote your conscience—or your district. But on the Rules Committee, if we need your vote, you'll give it to us—even if you hate the bill."[32]

More generally, Rayburn's knowledge of and effectiveness in the House meant that a good word from the Speaker could aid members in passing key legislation or in enhancing their influence in the overall legislative process. Both in passing legislation and in his influence throughout the Washington community and in the executive branch, Rayburn's preferment could help members bring beneficial projects home to their districts. Thus, if Rayburn lacked the power that Cannon had to influence the renomination of rank-and-file members, O'Neill claimed that "Sam had other ways to help a member get reelected. He'd call a committee chairman and say, 'I want you to put in a dam for this guy.' Or he'd call the Army Corps of Engineers and tell them, 'Start the canal on Monday. I've got a member who needs it.'"[33] Of course, these legislative influences on reelection were bolstered, too, by Rayburn's influence in the party and electoral system. Beginning with the 1940 congressional elections, Rayburn and Lyndon Johnson regularly tapped Texas oil interests for money to distribute to the campaigns of congressional Democrats. Through his Texas and national party ties, Rayburn maintained a reservoir of funds that would build loyalty among members.

The influence of these more tangible chits was reinforced by a more subtle and social system of preferment that could make the life of a member more commodious and prestigious on Capitol Hill. The Speaker's control over House administration and the House side of the Capitol grounds afforded him control of Capitol office space and renovations as well as hundreds of jobs on Capitol Hill, the allocation of which he could distribute to members as favors. Moreover, the Speaker could also bestow favors upon members by allowing them the highly visible honor of presiding over the House in the Speaker's absence or to chair the Committee of the Whole.[34] By the same token, Rayburn also controlled key appointments to various Boards on the Capitol, in the party, or in the District of Columbia that could raise a member's visibility and prestige.

Rayburn's multiple vantage points and resources made it difficult to resist a personal appeal from the Speaker; although Rayburn rarely punished members for not voting with him, the Speaker could often withhold key rewards and support. Even if the context of the House precluded strong, formal leadership on the basis of partisanship, Rayburn's informal style seems an effort to compensate for the lack of formal powers. Having examined the "thank you" notes and other papers in the Rayburn archives, one scholar concluded that Rayburn had nurtured an "economy of favors."[35] And Rayburn's close associate and protégé, Richard Bolling, used a similar metaphor claiming that Rayburn "accumulated a capital budget of personal influence that drew interest."[36]

Speaker Rayburn used his informed sense of the House to look for opportunities to strike bargains and to get legislation passed. At the same time, he knew when those opportunities were not available, and he sought to avoid conflicts. This position of informational strength allowed for what has been described as Rayburn's "light touch of leadership," in which he would not ask members to make votes that would hurt them in their districts. But this permissiveness, although a product of the relatively meager influence of leaders and seen by many as weakness, became a strength, as any request Rayburn made was deemed important and assumed to be reasonable. As one Democratic member of the time said of his party's leaders: "They do so little asking, in fact, that if they did ask me I'd do my darndest to go along with them."[37] Often Rayburn would make personal requests to members to vote with him if he needed their votes, as another member recounted:

> My district opposes the party position on farm policy. The Speaker called me and said, 'This is very vital to the party, particularly with the national election approaching. Can you possibly go along with us?' It was a personal appeal from the Speaker on the day of the vote. I told him that . . . if my vote would make the difference I would vote with him, but, if possible, I wanted to wait until the second round on the roll call and, if my vote was not needed, vote my district. He said, 'That is fine. That is all I want.' Friends told me he talked to them also. In effect he buttoned the thing up by that type of personal appeal.[38]

Rayburn frequently made use of these "pocket votes," whereby if the Speaker's position was likely to lose (or had lost on the first voting), a number of members would change their votes to provide the Speaker with a needed win.

The nature of the personal influence Rayburn developed is not simply a random enhancement of influence; rather it consisted of the building blocks of influence that were specifically targeted by Rayburn himself to aid the Speaker in meeting the role that the institutional context suggested. The prerogative powers that were left him, the strength of the committee system, the committee chairs, and the norms of committee deference, as well as the characteristics of the majority party he led all suggested that to be effective, Rayburn had to be a bargainer. But the Rayburn style should be remembered less for these limitations than for his strategic and effective adaptations to supplement his meager formal influence with informal resources and reputation.

## *Rayburn and Institutional Innovation*

In addition to legislative influence, another common test of the "greatness" of a legislative leader is that leader's ability and, indeed, willingness to change the institution by promoting institutional change or marshaling support for reform. Strahan, for instance, held out Speakers Henry Clay, Thomas Brackett Reed, and Newt Gingrich as examples of "consequential leaders" who ushered in "major policy and institutional changes in Congress."[39] But how would Sam Rayburn, a stabilizing force in House politics, compare with these leaders who were in one form or another offering revolutionary change to the House? And is it analytically useful to compare Rayburn, whose aims were to stabilize the institution, to these agents of change?

To consider these questions alongside any assessment of leader greatness, one needs to separate out a leader's ability to achieve institutional change when necessary from his/her willingness to engage in change. That is, a leader could be fully capable of executing change but unwilling because a potential change or reform would be too costly, not worth the effort, or deemed damaging to the institution. In most cases, Rayburn (as progressive as he could be in terms of policy) was conservative in his view of institutions and generally skeptical about change. One of Rayburn's oft-quoted aphorisms was, "Any jackass can kick down a barn, but it takes a good carpenter to build one."

In addition to this personal reluctance to bring about change, it is also worth noting that institutional reformers tend to engage in their efforts as a result of some incongruence between the institution in question and their policy or political aims. That is, institutional change is the result of friction between existing structure and strategic purpose.[40] In the case of Henry Clay, the House, its Speakership, and its committee system were inefficient to the workload demands on Congress and partisan ends that Clay himself pursued.[41] As for Reed, the dilatory motions and general obstructionism of House Democrats propelled the adoption of Reed's Rules to centralize power in the House majority and the Speakership and to make the House more effective. And Newt Gingrich's "revolution" was an effort to undo forty years of Democratic rule and put a Republican imprint on the structure of the House, all the while advancing his own policy and institutional influence.

Rayburn's task was different. Although he was sometimes frustrated with the legislative process as it existed in the House, Rayburn rarely sought institutional change as a means of asserting a greater role for himself in that process. No Clay or Reed (and certainly no Gingrich), Rayburn opted instead to stabilize the House and preserve its features as much as he could. Indeed, given both the deeply entrenched nature of the House context, embedded as it was in forty years of declining parties and institutional reforms, why seek change unlikely to happen? By the same token, given his mastery of the Speaker's role in the bar gaining context, the motivation for change was lacking.

There was no need for Rayburn to kick the House down. To the contrary, he was a great institutional patriot who loved the House and its traditions. Unlike so many "institutional innovators" who seek to change an institution out of frustration or an inability to meet goals, Rayburn was highly effective in the textbook Congress. Thus he sought to preserve its features and the House's autonomy. What follows is a brief consideration of three pushes for change with which Rayburn contended as Speaker. In the first two instances—the 1946 Legislative Reorganization Act and the push for broadcast coverage of House proceedings—Rayburn played the role of protector of the status quo, importantly in both instances preserving the House's bargaining culture and forestalling moves for greater partisanship and public openness. But an instance at the end of his career demonstrates that Rayburn was not consistently opposed to change when it was needed and when he believed it was in the best interest of the House and of the American political system in general. The third and final case examines Rayburn's role in propelling institutional change by championing the expansion of the House Committee on Rules in 1961, a reform which was an early precursor to the more open, partisan, and majoritarian House that would emerge in the 1970s and beyond.

*Legislative Reorganization Act of 1946.* Outside of the adoption of standing committees at the beginning of the nineteenth century and the adoption of Reeds Rules and other strong party reforms at the end of the nineteenth century, there has been no more significant formal reform of the House's internal operations than the 1946 Legislative Reorganization Act. With this act, Congress decreased the number of committees, consolidated their power, and provided for increases in staff and other institutional resources that would help Congress meet the demands of a more robust and bureaucratized Washington politics. Along with the Administrative Procedures Act of the same year, the Legislative Reorganization Act represents Congress's efforts to modernize Congress and the executive branch so as to adjust existing institutions to the vast changes in policy and politics ushered in by Franklin Roosevelt's New Deal.

But the Reorganization bill that became law was not the same bill presented to the House by the Senate. The bill passed the Senate first with these consolidating and institutionalizing reforms as well as an additional element that would have transformed the role of party in Congress by establishing partisan "policy committees" that would increase the ability of Congress to form an agenda, coordinate between the chambers, and deal with the executive branch. Even if the bulk of the changes reinforced the power centers of Rayburn's House and helped to facilitate the kind of rule that he brought to the institution, Rayburn slowed its progress over these more transformative elements that would have increased "party responsibility."[42] As Hardeman and Bacon observed, Rayburn's

> main objection was a provision creating majority and minority policy committees. These panels were designed to strengthen party responsibility and accountability, but Rayburn saw them as unnecessary and perhaps even damaging to the strong Democratic leadership he exercised. The Democratic policy committee would have responsibility for scheduling legislation and for disciplining recalcitrant members.[43]

To be sure, Rayburn had his own belief in party and party responsibility, but he believed the establishment of party "policy committees" to be a bridge too far. Dissatisfied with the redundancy of his own functions in the House and the potential disruption that such party councils might cause, Rayburn "refused to send it to committee or discuss further movement until its supporters agreed to certain changes."[44]

Rayburn's objections are telling. First, having formalized party committees performing these essential functions was undoubtedly a threat to Rayburn's own power and authority. Legislative scheduling and "disciplining recalcitrant members" (if he would choose to do so) were leadership functions not to be surrendered to a committee. Second, Rayburn's effectiveness as leader rested, in large part, on the avoidance of intra-party conflict and the management of the party agenda to circumvent rifts. To subject the House Democratic Party to regular bouts of discord was one of the chief reasons that the party had let the caucus fall into disuse and surely would have wreaked more havoc for the deeply divided Democratic majority than for the more unified Republican minority. Third, the open airing of intra-party disputes promised by such party policy committees would simply have decreased the information advantages that Rayburn had accumulated in the decentralized system of the textbook Congress.

So what passed and what was left to languish by virtue of Rayburn's action on the Legislative Reorganization Act? What was made law was the consolidation of committee power and a more complete funding of the House as an institution. What was eliminated, largely by Rayburn's hand, were the elements that would challenge the party leader-committee chair collaborations that marked the textbook era and at which Rayburn was practiced and effective. Thus, in regard to institutional change, the Reorganization Act is a complex case. The changes that emerged made the Legislative Reorganization Act a reinforcement of the textbook Congress's bargaining culture rather than a reform of it. The elements of the Senate bill that posed the greatest challenge to the House's bargaining culture languished on Rayburn's desk until their proponents relented. As one characterization of the outcome put it, "The Reorganization bill which finally passed the House actually contained more than the Senate expected to get, but it still bore the mark of Sam Rayburn. It was illustrative of his technique as a compromiser, his ability to get men to work together congenially."[45] It was illustrative, too, of Rayburn's willingness to preserve the key elements of the House and its bargaining culture even at a time of significant institutional change and formal reorganization.

*Broadcast Coverage of the House.* Changes less formal than the statutory reforms of the Legislative Reorganization Act also represented a threat to the bargaining culture of the House that Rayburn prized and in which he thrived. A consequence of Rayburn's longevity in politics is that his congressional career saw the rise of both radio and television as political forces. As politicians used these media technologies increasingly in their own campaigns, they pushed for greater access of broadcast media to the House itself.

If Rayburn was a relatively junior member when radio transformed the American political landscape in the 1920s and 1930s, he was Speaker by the time television was emerging as a political force. As television became more important to American politics in the 1950s, elements within Congress sought to open up the Senate and the House, respectively, to broadcast media. Members seeking reelection would look for opportunities to publicize their official actions. Committees and committee chairs seeking publicity for their legislative and political aims looked to television to broadcast their high profile, sometimes spectacular, hearings and investigations. Again, Rayburn resisted the change by trying to control the flow of information and keep the internal workings of the House out of the limelight.

Rayburn's resistance to television politics in the House was overdetermined, as multiple factors made the speaker skeptical of the new medium. First, Rayburn believed that it was difficult to translate the hard work of legislative politics to the public through broadcast media. Like many of his House contemporaries, Rayburn made a distinction between the "workhorses" who wrote legislation and did the hard work of the legislature and the "showhorses" who played to the cameras and claimed credit for legislative accomplishments. Rayburn's antipathy toward the House's showhorses was clear when he said, "Damn the fellow who's always seeking publicity."[46] And, he believed that televised Senate hearings had "made ham actors out of ambitious Senators."[47]

Second, television would expose the legislative process to press and public scrutiny in ways that were likely to distort operations and disrupt progress. Thinking that television would change the House's information economy and spur the potential for the kinds of grandstanding and partisan posturing that would preclude bargaining, Rayburn preferred to keep things relatively quiet, and he used his position to keep the press, particularly the broadcast media, out. Rayburn strictly enforced House rules against broadcast coverage of House proceedings.[48] His reluctance to allow broadcast of the House were put most explicitly in a 1952 interview. Rayburn said:

> I am of the opinion that [television coverage is] not helpful either to the Committees of Congress or to the public in general. They slow up proceedings of Committees and lengthen them, and the parts that are put on television are only the so-called 'high-lights' that do not give a good demonstration of Committee proceedings or a clear picture of the issues. I do not think it is conducive to decorum or orderly procedure to have flash bulb pictures being taken or television cameras in operation while a Committee is in actual hearing. I have found, after long experience, that these are disturbing factors, and few Members of Congress want these things to happen.[49]

Put more succinctly, Rayburn said, "If we allowed the televising of everything that comes along up here we would never get anything done."[50]

Third, echoing his concerns about "decorum" in the above quotation, Rayburn believed that television would harm the House's reputation, and he used his position to rein in more public House leaders. When rogue committee chairs attempted to circumvent House rules regarding broadcast coverage of committee proceedings, Rayburn used his influence to stop each transgressor. Upon hearing of one such attempt, Rayburn wrote to his Executive Assistant Robert Bartley, "I have been told that at one time Cecil King [Ways and Means Subcommittee chair] had agreed to set up television in his Committee. I am expecting you and [House Parliamentarian] Lew Deschler to handle this. I have given no authority to him or anybody else to set up television in the House of Representatives, and I do not want it started by King or anyone else."[51] And when Representative Francis E. 'Tad' Walter (D-PA), Chairman of the House Un-American Activities Committee and friend of Rayburn, held televised committee meetings in June of 1957, Rayburn immediately wired Walter to cease and desist and summoned the HUAC Chairman to explain his actions. Upon Walter's return he met with Rayburn, and one Rayburn aide said, "I don't know what Mr. Rayburn said, but when Mr. Walter emerged to the outer office, he was as white and shaken as I never saw him before or since." After the meeting Rayburn simply told reporters, "Tad Walter is not going to televise any meetings anymore."[52]

Fourth and finally, it is worth pointing out that televising House proceedings promised to make for an all-too-public airing of internecine disagreements, the likes of which the Rayburn style sought to contain. If the hallmarks of Rayburn's efforts to manage information in the House included taciturnity, compartmentalization, and the avoidance of policy conflicts within the deeply divided Democratic Party, then television was a potent threat to the House political system that Rayburn commanded. Indeed, if the airing of policy disagreements in closed caucus meetings or internal institutional policy committees, as suggested in the Senate version of the Legislative Reorganization Act, was too potentially damaging, then what would televising committee or floor proceedings do to Rayburn's fragile and bifurcated coalition? As with the Legislative Reorganization Act, in the case of the potential broadcasting of House proceedings, Rayburn resisted innovation in an effort to preserve the House institution he knew and its effectiveness as he understood it.

Notably, Rayburn's hard line on broadcast coverage included resistance to dramatic calls to address the issue. On the House floor, for instance, there were calls as early as 1955 to fully eliminate the House Un-American Activities Committee, but Rayburn avoided joining those calls and cited Chief Justice Earl Warren's denouncement of the committee's seeking "exposure for the sake of exposure."[53] Even when fighting to preserve the House, Rayburn looked for ways to avoid direct conflict.

*Expansion of the Rules Committee.* Whereas Rayburn protected committee and leader autonomy from tenets of the Legislative Reorganization Act and from the burgeoning force of television, he ended his career fighting for a key reform that would be a harbinger of a more partisan and less committee-dominated House to come.

After John F. Kennedy's narrow presidential victory in 1960, questions quickly emerged about the degree to which he would command support among Democrats in Congress. Particularly in the House, where Democrats had lost seats in the 1960 election and southern conservatives still dominated committees, the passage of Kennedy's New Frontier was uncertain to say the least. Even more damaging to the Democrats' and the House's reputation, an alliance of southern Democrats and Republicans on the House Committee on Rules, led by Chairman Howard Smith (D-VA), made it unlikely that key elements of Kennedy's legislative program would even get to be voted on the House floor.

When the majority's ability to control the legislative agenda was threatened by Chairman Howard Smith and the conservative coalition, and, indeed, when the Kennedy program faced defeat, Rayburn used his sense of the House and his considerable bargaining skills and resources to build the coalition that would take the unusual step to expand the Rules Committee. *Even if Rayburn's long-standing position was to resist change, he was more pro-House than he was anti-reform.* Thus, when change, even radical change, proved necessary to keep the House an effective legislative body, Rayburn would lead the charge. Nowhere was this more in evidence than in Rayburn's effort to expanding the House Committee on Rules in 1961.

In an epic battle between Rayburn in the last year of his life and Chairman Smith, another titan of the House, Rayburn worked with liberals to expand the size of the House Committee on Rules from twelve to fifteen members. The intended effect of this change was to wrest control of the committee from a conservative coalition of southern Democrats and minority party Republicans who opposed Kennedy's legislative agenda, and to make it so that the Kennedy program would reach the House floor for votes, and the House majority party Democrats, in the face of conservative opposition, could increase their influence in the legislative process. After weeks of planning and reputedly Herculean efforts to move votes, Rayburn was victorious by a vote of 217 to 212 over Smith's formidable alliance.

This was Rayburn's final great act as an institutional innovator. Still, even when Rayburn was at the forefront of institutional change, he was loath to be anything other than a defender of the traditional institutional context of the House. The Speaker went to considerable lengths to avoid disruptive change to the Rules Committee. In prior Congresses, Rayburn sought to use his connections to Minority Leader Joe Martin to pick up Republican votes on Rules to counteract Democratic defections. After Representative Charles Halleck's successful bid to unseat Martin as minority leader, this remedy was foreclosed. And it was at that point that "Rayburn reluctantly decided to move to change the political balance of the Rules Committee."[54] Prior to early 1961, it was Rayburn's effectiveness in prying legislation out of Rules that precluded the need for more significant and enduring institutional change.

By the same token, the plan to expand the Committee on Rules rather than displace recalcitrant members was part of Rayburn's attempt to respect the norms of the House of Representatives. Representative William Colmer (D-MS), along with Chairman Smith, had consistently allied himself with Rules Committee Republicans. At a meeting of top Democratic leaders in the first days of 1961, according to Richard Bolling, more than one Rayburn lieutenant offered that "the disloyal southern Democrats such as Colmer must be purged because moderate Southerners could not long afford to be identified with them," but "Rayburn, not surprisingly, demurred."[55] Rather than purge anyone, Rayburn opted instead to expand the committee so that he could appoint loyal Democrats to tip the balance of power. This plan was, in Rayburn's words, "the way to embarrass nobody if they don't want to be embarrassed."[56]

Indeed, compromise and the avoidance of conflict were typical of Rayburn's modus operandi. By the end of January and beginning of February 1961, when the Kennedy administration was contacting Democratic members for support and Whip Carl Albert and other key Democrats were rounding up votes, Rayburn was entertaining compromise. Cummings and Peabody claim that "Rayburn might have been willing to call off the vote [on expanding the committee] if he could have obtained Smith's written guarantee that the Rules Committee would not block any Kennedy legislative proposal during the coming session."[57] Only after exhausting potential alternatives and when pressures from an increasingly liberal House Democratic Party and a sense that the House should be able to "work its will" on the Kennedy program did Rayburn ultimately advocate the institutional innovation of committee expansion.

In his floor speech advocating passage of the resolution, Rayburn said, "We have elected to the Presidency a new leader. He is going to have a program that he thinks will be in the interest of and for the benefit of the American people. . . . Let us move this program. Let us be sure we can move it and the only way we can be sure that this program will move when great committees report bills, the only way it can move, in my opinion, my beloved colleagues, is to adopt this resolution today."[58] Ultimately, Rayburn's plea (along with his legendary behind-the-scenes efforts) proved successful at expanding the Committee on Rules. Still, in typical Rayburn fashion, the enlargement of the committee avoided "final resolution" on many "underlying issues," as Peabody and Cummings put it, that would require longer-term institutional innovation:

> Rayburn opted for the positive course of action that created the minimum disturbance possible in the *status quo*. No attack was made on the committee's jurisdiction or powers. No member was unseated, nor was party discipline applied. Even the resolution to enlarge the committee was worded so as to apply to the Eighty-Seventh Congress only.[59]

Rayburn's battle to expand the Rules Committee is, in many ways, an exceptional moment in his Speakership. Credited with successfully challenging the conservative coalition, a dominant committee chairman, and doing so aggressively in the interest of the administration and the partisan majority in the House, Rayburn achieved a dramatic and narrow victory in his last major battle in the House. In some ways, this battle was a precursor to a later era of congressional politics that Speaker Rayburn would miss. Still, the Speaker saw the writing on the wall. Southern committee chair dominance of the House was unsustainable as the country continued to change, the parties grew increasingly polarized, and the Democratic Party became more liberal. But even in this exceptional instance, Rayburn's first inclinations were to avoid conflict, seek out acceptable compromises, and opt for institutional change only as a last resort.

## *Conclusions: The House in Rayburn's Wake*

The dominant characteristics of the Rayburn style of leadership were the informal innovations and behaviors he engaged in to be effective within the bargaining context of the House. Rayburn built a successful and accomplished speakership despite the comparative weakness of his office and the internal divisions of his party in the mid-twentieth century. Indeed, so successful was Rayburn in this role that he resisted most opportunities for institutional reform, opting instead to preserve the status quo. Unlike other leaders who might seek to transform the institution, Rayburn cultivated informal resources to maximize his effectiveness in the role determined by the institutional context.

Still, it should be obvious to any contemporary reader that Rayburn's House and his leadership are far afield from the roles and functions performed by contemporary leaders, and his efforts to forestall institutional change were overtaken by historical forces that produced a much more partisan, polarized, and open Congress after the reforms of the 1970s. The context of the House changed. The Democratic Party, once divided by north and south, would lose much of its southern contingent beginning in the 1960s and continuing to present day, making the Democrats more unified and liberal and the Republicans more southern, more unified, and conservative. As a result, institutional reforms of the 1970s broke up the committee baronies, dispersed power throughout the House membership, and multiplied the number of important players in House politics. And, by the same token, sunshine reforms that opened up the House to press and public scrutiny, including C-SPAN, challenged the House's bargaining and compromise cultures. The key elements of the Rayburn context—a divided party, committee dominance, and a House insulated from its environment—had eroded, if slowly, and despite Rayburn's own efforts to preserve them.

All told, these changes made the bargainer role of the Speaker outmoded, impractical, and unworkable. And this has come at some considerable detriment of Congress and the country. Accommodation, bargaining, and compromise would give way to polarization, posturing, and gridlock. The strategic agents of this new era—Gingrich, Pelosi, Tom DeLay, Kevin McCarthy, and John Boehner, to name a few—are un-Rayburn like. They take to the airwaves and the Internet to propel partisanship;[60] they rail against the opposition party and even question its loyalty; and they seemingly put partisan interests over the best interests of the country as a matter of course. Rather than seeking to make a government run, they would opt instead to shut it down to make a point or hold merely symbolic votes in vain to repeal legislation instead of offering their own legislative paths forward. Scholars should continue to debate if these leaders deserve blame or if this is all that strategic agents can do in such a transformed and polarized context.

Regardless of the outcome of that debate, this state of affairs makes it quite likely that Sam Rayburn's place in the pantheon of the House's greatest leaders is in no jeopardy from today's leaders. Contemporary leaders, by virtue of their partisanship, are likely to be strong and even impactful partisans but, ultimately, they will be weak leaders, protectors, and preservers of the House and the country. They may, in fact, impress many congressional leadership scholars and confirm the discipline's dominant theories of party leader strength in partisan eras, but today's congressional leaders are likely to be meager in individual impact and low in terms of historical consequence.

Clifford Barryman cartoon depicting President Harry Truman and his close friend Sam Rayburn coping with post-WWII difficulties six months into Truman's service as president. *Collection of the Library of Congress.*

# 7

# Sam Rayburn's Presidents

## *Institutional, Party, and Personal Power Relationships*

Douglas B. Harris and Garrison Nelson

Sam Rayburn famously argued that he had "served with" but "never under" eight presidents, ranging from Woodrow Wilson to John F. Kennedy. First elected to the House in 1912, he arrived in Washington with Wilson's first administration and remained there until his death in 1961. This remarkable longevity included serving as Speaker of the House for seventeen of twenty-one years, from 1940 to his death in 1961—that is, from Franklin Roosevelt's presidency into that of John F. Kennedy.[1] Working with Presidents Wilson, Harding, Coolidge, Hoover, and Franklin Roosevelt before entering the House leadership, Rayburn became Speaker during Roosevelt's presidency and worked, as Speaker of the House, with Presidents Truman, Eisenhower, and Kennedy. As Speaker, Rayburn was on the front lines of governing in the mid-twentieth century and was a stabilizing force in American national politics amid the New Deal, World War II, Korea, the Cold War, and the beginnings of the civil rights era.

No doubt Rayburn's observation that he never served "under" a President of the United States reflected his institutional patriotism for the House of Representatives and his traditionalist sense that Congress is a coequal branch of government. Having served as a major committee chair during the early New Deal, as House majority leader in 1937, and as Speaker beginning in 1940, Rayburn was a top legislative leader for all of Franklin Roosevelt's presidency, making him an important player in the New Deal's historic legislative accomplishments and an important consolidator and defender of its policy gains for Roosevelt's presidency and thereafter. Indeed, as an influential partner in governing, Rayburn played key roles in defending the New Deal both from the internal strains of the New Deal coalition during the Truman administration and from a Republican effort to slow Democratic trends during the divided government of the Eisenhower years.[2] Although slowed by age and sickness during the first year of the Kennedy administration, Rayburn fought a titanic battle to unleash the legislative program of the New Frontier from the confines of a reluctant House Rules Committee and generally played a role as senior counselor to the young President Kennedy.

Crucial to the Democratic and national politics of the mid-twentieth century, Rayburn's relationships with these presidents were critical to America's domestic policy developments and foreign policy accomplishments. An initial aim of this chapter is to situate Sam Rayburn's relationships with these presidents in the context of broader patterns of inter-branch politics. Going beyond mere same-party/different-party observations of Speaker-president relationships, this chapter seeks to provide an exhaustive list of potential relationships between Speakers and presidents that reflects how inter-branch as well as personal power differentials might also affect the relationship between these two constitutional offices, and then to apply those models to Sam Rayburn's relationships with the four presidents with whom he served as Speaker.

More than simply testing a typology that we are creating to examine Speaker-president relationships throughout American political history, we believe that this framework will help to shed light on the personal and power relationships Rayburn had with Roosevelt, Truman, Eisenhower, and Kennedy, respectively. Knowing how Rayburn interacted with these presidents and examining the primary considerations that seem to explain his behavior when he interacted with the White House allows for a better understanding of Rayburn's own leadership style, his institutional role as he performed it, and his importance to American political history.

## *Modeling President-Speaker Relationships*

In broader examinations of the relationship between Speakers and Presidents, we have identified a three-variable matrix that, we believe, illuminates the Speaker-President relationship. This matrix examines:

1) The party control of the presidency and the House of Representatives: *is there unified or divided party control?*
2) The relative balance of power between the institutions led by respective presidents and Speakers during the years of any given President-Speaker pairing: *is the power balanced between the presidency and the House in terms of domestic policy-making or is there an imbalance favoring one of the institutions?*
3) If there is an imbalance of power, *is the president dominant or is the Speaker dominant*? By contrast, if institutional power is balanced, *is the Speaker-President relationship cooperative or competitive?*

Applying these three questions to the President-Speaker relationships throughout American history produces eight potential models of this constitutional separation of powers relationship. If the president and the Speaker are from the same party, the president or Speaker could be institutionally dominant, or, if the offices are relatively balanced, then their relationship could be either primarily cooperative or competitive, though the party context might suggest that cooperation would be more likely. By the same token, if the president and the Speaker are from different parties, either office still could be institutionally dominant, and, again, if the offices are relatively balanced in power, the relationship, though likely to be partisan and competitive, could under some conditions be cooperative.

Notably, there are historical examples that fit well each of these hypothesized models. Examples of *Unified President Dominant* relationships include Andrew Jackson and Speaker Andrew Stevenson (1827–1834) or George W. Bush and J. Dennis Hastert (2001–2006). Occasionally, Speakers have dominated presidents of their own party; *Unified Speaker Dominant* relationships might include James Madison and Henry Clay, or Ulysses S. Grant and James Blaine. When Speakers and presidents of the same party are balanced in power, they can either be primarily cooperative as were Bill Clinton and Tom Foley (*Unified Balanced Cooperative*) or primarily competitive like Teddy Roosevelt and Joseph Cannon (*Unified Balanced Competitive*).

Although some of the aforementioned Speakers were prominent

and even among the greatest Speakers in House history, it is divided party control that enhances a Speaker's importance and public prominence. Examples of *Divided President Dominant* relationships might include Harry Truman and Joe Martin or Richard Nixon and John McCormack. Occasionally, a Speaker might dominate a president during divided government (*Divided Speaker Dominant*), as did Thomas Brackett Reed during Grover Cleveland's administration, Jim Wright in the last two years of the Reagan administration, or Newt Gingrich over Bill Clinton in the wake of the 1994 Republican Revolution. Finally, divided party control of the presidency and the House can produce *Divided Balanced Cooperative* relationships like Nixon and Albert just prior to Watergate or *Divided Balanced Competitive* relationships like Hoover and John Nance Garner during the Seventy-Second Congress or George H. W. Bush and Tom Foley during the 102nd Congress.

Where do Sam Rayburn's relationships with his four presidents fit in? Rayburn served as Speaker with three presidents of his own party—Franklin Roosevelt, Harry Truman, and John F. Kennedy—and with one Republican President, Dwight Eisenhower. In most cases, the Rayburn era was typified by a relative balance of presidential and congressional power, and we categorize Rayburn as being in a *Unified Balanced Cooperative* relationship with both Roosevelt and Truman and a *Divided Balanced Cooperative* relationship with Eisenhower. With Kennedy, Rayburn was certainly cooperative, but the imbalance in experience and the centrality of Rayburn's efforts to expand the Rules Committee to Kennedy's ultimate legislative success in the first year likely indicates that this relationship was that of *Unified Speaker Dominant*.

This is not to say that there are no gradations among the power relationships he had with presidents. Rayburn was, for example, much more deferential to Roosevelt than to Truman or especially Kennedy. Still, when compared to Roosevelt's relationships with Henry Rainey or Joseph Byrns (*Unified President Dominant*), Rayburn was much more of an active participant in Roosevelt's achievements than a rubber stamp. Readers should note, too, that our characterization of Rayburn's relationship with Eisenhower as *cooperative* does not ignore the significant partisan and policy conflicts that existed between the two during the 1950s, key elements of which we will explore below.[3]

In all, it is worth noting that Rayburn was more effective than both his predecessors and successors in the Speakership and, to a president, he was the most effective and influential Speaker with whom any of them served. Rayburn was the fourth Speaker with whom Franklin Roosevelt served, but his relationship with the president was far better and on a more even level than that of Speakers Henry Rainey, Joseph Byrns, or William Bankhead. Both Rainey and Byrns, Speakers from 1933 to 1934 and from 1935 to 1936, respectively, were in failing health (indeed, each died in his brief Speakership), but also served at the height of Roosevelt's power during his first term. Speaker William Bankhead was Speaker during FDR's second term, when key divisions within the Democratic coalition would reemerge, and the fault lines in Roosevelt's popularity would become more obvious, especially concerning efforts to pack the Supreme Court in 1937 or purge conservative Democrats in the 1938 primary elections. As a result, Bankhead was more useful and more forceful in his relationship with Roosevelt than Rainey or Byrns had been, or could have been. It was even truer of Rayburn, whose effectiveness would make him arguably even more of an equal partner with FDR than Bankhead, owing in part to Bankhead's poor health throughout his time as Speaker.

There is no question that Rayburn was the most effective Speaker with whom Roosevelt served, which was true also of presidents Truman, Eisenhower, and Kennedy. Truman served not only with Rayburn as Speaker but also with Joe Martin, Republican of Massachusetts, when Republicans took control of the House in the Eightieth Congress. Whereas Rayburn and Truman worked closely together in a cooperative and balanced relationship, Martin arguably took a backseat, particularly with Rayburn serving effectively as minority leader. The same was true of Martin's second stint as Speaker during the first two years of the Eisenhower administration. There is no doubt that Martin was a stalwart supporter of Eisenhower, but the president's honeymoon and great popularity (he was always more popular than the Republican Party he led) meant that Eisenhower was dominant. By contrast, during the last six years of Eisenhower's two terms, Sam Rayburn, returned to the Speakership, was a closely balanced and mostly cooperative partisan foil for the president. But Rayburn's interaction with all of these presidents is more complex than placement in any model could capture. Personally, institutionally, and in regard to the party balance, Rayburn's interactions with each of his presidents was a strategic response to multiple factors as they changed and interacted over time and varied by context.

## *Rayburn and the Presidents With Whom He Served*

Personally, Rayburn was known for a leadership style that included personal qualities such as comity and affect.[4] Personal relationships and personal affection seemed to typify most of Rayburn's interactions with the presidents with whom he served as Speaker. Still, Rayburn's personal ties to various presidents operated in the context of the broader institutional and partisan roles that each played. In the case of Truman, for example, Rayburn was a close personal friend with the president, and this reinforced the cooperative relationship between the Democratic Speaker and the Democratic White House. In the case of Eisenhower, by contrast, the intimation of a personal relationship was often used to deflect the conflict between the two men, their offices, and their parties.

As Speaker, Rayburn was *the* representative of the House of Representatives to actors in the other branches of government and, to a lesser degree, to the public at large. By extension, he was an institutional patriot to the core, and he defended the autonomy and influence of the House of Representatives in the separation of powers framework. This is not to say that he was uncompromising in separation of powers interaction. As much as Rayburn would protect the House and deny that he ever "served under" any president, he was nevertheless cooperative and perhaps deferential, in part. As Rayburn protégé Dick Bolling put it, "Rayburn was very interesting in his relationship to all presidents. He felt that while he might disagree with them, that the President ought to have his chance."[5]

Sam Rayburn was an institution in and of himself, a fixture in both the Washington community and a leader (and symbol) of the Democratic Party that he led. By virtue of his longevity, his character and consistency, Rayburn was widely liked and respected in the Washington community. His personal commitments to populism and to the Democratic Party fed his policy views and his willingness to engage in partisan conflict, but generally to do so without personalizing the conflict or becoming disagreeable. Ultimately, his pragmatism, patriotism, and love of the House meant that partisan considerations would often take a back seat to considerations of what was possible to pass and what was in the best interest, long-term, of the House and the nation.

## *The New Speaker and the New Deal: Rayburn and FDR*

Rayburn rose to prominence during Franklin Roosevelt's presidency, a fact that colored his relationship with the president. In short, Rayburn admired Roosevelt and was deferential and supportive. But as Roosevelt's presidency turned in the late 1930s from legislative expansion to protecting gains made in the early years and then to foreign policy, Rayburn's position in the House was elevated, and his partnership with Roosevelt approached parity.

Valuable to Roosevelt from the beginning, Rayburn began the New Deal era as chairman of the Committee on Interstate and Foreign Commerce, a post that he had held since Democrats regained majority control in the aftermath of the 1930 elections. Given the importance of the Constitution's interstate commerce clause to many efforts to expand federal power, Rayburn was at the center of the action for much of the New Deal legislative agenda; in the first years of Roosevelt's presidency, Rayburn "co-authored five major pieces of legislation: the Emergency Railroad Transportation Act, the Truth in Securities Act, the Stock Exchange Act [Securities Exchange Act], the Federal Communications Act, and . . . the Public Utility Holding Company Act," accomplishments which would be followed by the Rural Electrification Act, which was also central to the New Deal's domestic aims.[6]

Rayburn moved quickly into higher leadership positions during Roosevelt's second term. When Speaker Joseph Byrns died in 1936, Majority Leader William Bankhead succeeded to the Speakership, thus sparking a race for the Democratic floor leader's spot. Although other candidates were mentioned, the race quickly was reduced to a contest between Rayburn and Rules Committee Chairman John O'Connor of New York. If O'Connor was a northern Democrat (from New York City) and brother to Roosevelt's law partner, he was also considered an opponent of key New Deal legislation, whereas Rayburn was a productive champion of New Deal policy. Thus, even if the administration thought that Rayburn was "too cautious" and "too slow to move" for FDR's tastes,[7] he was far superior to O'Connor. Key administration members and Roosevelt supporters, including Vice President John Nance Garner and the DNC Chairman Jim Farley, campaigned for Rayburn. So widespread was the view that FDR was supporting Rayburn that when Roosevelt issued a statement declaring his neutrality in internal House leadership races, O'Connor celebrated the neutrality in a statement and the Rayburn forces, as O'Connor complained, continued to "wink" that this was not the case.[8] In retrospect, it seems clear that FDR preferred Rayburn over O'Connor; indeed, O'Connor would be the only successful object of Roosevelt's 1938 purge effort.

Rayburn's succession to the Speakership upon Bankhead's death in 1940 continued and deepened the alliance between Rayburn and FDR. They were close and respected one another. Upon becoming majority leader, Sam Rayburn worked with Roosevelt throughout most of his elongated presidency. "I sat across the desk from Roosevelt from 1937 until he died, every Monday morning for an hour," said Rayburn.[9] The relationship was, at times, warm and jovial. On the occasion of Rayburn's sixtieth birthday, Franklin Roosevelt summoned the Speaker to the White House (for the purposes of a surprise party); McCormack joined Rayburn, but "when the President was ready he asked Mr. Rayburn to come in alone and the Speaker said, 'I have no secrets from John McCormack.'" Rayburn would find out that the visit was simply to celebrate Rayburn's birthday and that McCormack had known of the surprise.[10]

Still, the shared commitments of the Texas populist and the New York aristocrat to the Democratic Party and its constituents was the glue that forged the bonds between the two men. Looking back on FDR, Rayburn recalled witnessing the president's personal commitment to the poor and the working class in America; the Speaker said, "Roosevelt was really for the underdog. And the people knew it, and that is why they loved and revered Roosevelt."[11]

With common policy goals, Rayburn worked closely with the administration to plan strategy and to move legislation. Rayburn intimate Richard Bolling recalled that both Tommy "the Cork" Corcoran and Ben Cohen worked closely with Rayburn to advance New Deal bills through the legislative process.[12] Still, FDR continued to be more aggressive than Rayburn. In a letter to Rayburn in December 1940 following his third election, and on the eve of the upcoming Seventy-Seventh Congress, Roosevelt counseled Sam Rayburn and Majority

Leader John McCormack to engage in "'fighting leadership,' with the adjective 'fighting' underscored:"

> What I want to get across to both of you before the new session begins is that good fellowship for the sake of good fellowship alone, an easy life to avoid criticism, an acceptance of defeat before an issue has been joined, make, all of them, less for Party success and for national safety than a few drag-down and knock-out fights and an unwillingness to accept defeat without a fight.[13]

Roosevelt's cajoling of Rayburn and McCormack to be more aggressive is consistent with his overall attempts to be more aggressive in taking the Democratic Party to the left. His efforts to change the structure of the Democratic Party by eliminating the two-thirds rule in 1936, his court-packing attempts in 1937, and his largely failed purge of conservatives from the party in 1938 were are all signs of a Roosevelt restless for change and a more programmatically liberal Democratic Party.[14]

But this was not to be. The failed nature of the purge meant that many southern Democrats returned to Congress piqued by Roosevelt's move against them and no longer willing to support the president as a matter of course. Indeed, with an antagonized southern Democratic party, the best the administration could hope for was to protect the gains made.[15] Thus, in many ways, Rayburn's caution, his experience, and his ability to reach out to southerners as well as northerners was key to the maintenance of the New Deal legacy and the protection of its new policies. According to biographers Hardeman and Bacon, Rayburn established himself as a "dependable ally" for the president: "If Roosevelt still did not accept Congress as an equal, at least he was beginning to see the value in closer cooperation and compromise."[16]

FDR's reliance on Rayburn grew and was necessitated by a number of factors. First, America would soon be gearing up for World War II. Speaker Rayburn and Majority Leader John McCormack were central to Roosevelt's legislative efforts in the run-up to the war. Key legislation such as Lend-Lease, the Draft Extension, and the Repeal of the Neutrality Acts owed much to the efforts of the House leaders. Perhaps nothing more epitomized the pre-war Roosevelt-Rayburn alliance than how Sam Rayburn's quick gavel secured the one-vote passage of the Draft Extension Act of 1941. As described by FDR biographer Conrad Black, "The President had Speaker Sam Rayburn to thank for getting it through at all, by gaveling down attempted vote changes and recounts."[17] Second, the political toll of the war and the midterm elections of 1942 weakened the Democrats' numbers in Congress and emboldened a conservative coalition in opposition to Roosevelt's more progressive forays. If the alliance of southern Democrats with Republicans blunted FDR's efforts to expand the reach of the national government further still, the firm control of the House by Rayburn and McCormack (along with their counterparts in the Senate) protected the New Deal's initial policy gains from retrenchment and repeal. And, third, the difficulty of prosecuting the war required levels of unity and bipartisanship that were more Rayburn's wheelhouse than Roosevelt's, who up to the beginning of the war had been a controversial figure among Republicans and who became more controversial among many southern conservative Democrats after court-packing and the 1938 purge effort.

Overall, Rayburn was a formidable ally as Roosevelt protected his domestic policy agenda from a conservative counteroffensive and as the president led the US in World War II. Rayburn's reputation inside the House, both with committee chairmen and with Minority Leader Joe Martin and other Republicans, helped FDR secure "the basic laws he needed to strengthen the war effort."[18] Nowhere was Rayburn's influence more important than in his efforts to help FDR secure a secret, "inscrutable" appropriation to fund the development of the atomic bomb. Early in 1944, General George Marshall, Secretary of War Henry Stimson, and Dr. Vannevar Bush came to Rayburn's office with news that the Germans were pursuing the technology to deploy an atomic weapon. Rayburn used his influence with tight-fisted Appropriations Chairman Clarence Cannon to secure a "secret" appropriation and tapped his relationship with Minority Leader Joe Martin to secure bipartisan cooperation on the committee and the floor. With Rayburn's influence, the administration was able to provide hundreds of millions of dollars to fund the atomic bomb project without the public or the enemy becoming aware.[19] Even as Rayburn worked with the executive branch to ensure secrecy for this key component of the war effort, it was his command of Congress and his reputation among colleagues that allowed him to remain a partner in such top-secret efforts, a fact which meant that Congress kept a (perhaps distant) hand in war-making, even during a presidency-dominant era. Through his work, his accomplishments, and his relationship with Roosevelt, Sam Rayburn asserted Congress's role domestically at a time when the presidency was on the rise.

## *Friends in Power: Rayburn and Truman*

Sam Rayburn and Harry Truman were close personal friends and thus their Speaker-President relationship was more balanced, perhaps even tipping in Rayburn's favor, as a result of the Speaker's longevity and experience, particularly his experience with Roosevelt. Truman had joined the Senate in 1935, more than two decades after Sam Rayburn had joined the House. While Truman was a relatively junior senator, Rayburn had worked closely with the White House since the beginning of the New Deal and especially since 1937.

In point of fact, Truman advocated Rayburn for vice president in 1944 and went to that year's convention in support of the Speaker's candidacy, only to become the nominee himself.[20] Rayburn, however, "prevailed" in conversation with Truman, convincing him to accede to the nomination and then working to secure the support of the Texas delegation for Truman's addition to Roosevelt's 1944 ticket. [21]

On April 12, 1945, less than three months after FDR's fourth inauguration, Vice President Truman was summoned to the White House to learn of FDR's death while socializing with Rayburn in the Speaker's Board of Education. It was their personal closeness and philosophical congruity that guaranteed their joint commitment to complete FDR's war effort and to manage the postwar agenda.

Truman's respect for Rayburn was great, and he had come to think of the Speaker as a mentor. Truman recounted their early relationship a few years later while on his 1948 whistle-stop campaign. To citizens in Bells, Texas, Truman said of Rayburn (who had introduced him):

> Sam is one of my friends who showed me around Washington the first time I ever went there, and I will never forget it. And his advice was, of course, sound and solid. He was always on the right side of the question, and I don't think I know a man in the Government of the United States who has done more for his country than Sam Rayburn.[22]

Later in Austin he sounded similar sentiments, saying, "Sam's been my friend ever since I've been in Washington, and when Sam's your friend, you're in pretty good shape in Washington—I can tell you that."[23]

This had been true since Truman's rise within the Democratic ranks and throughout his presidency. And with his sudden elevation to the presidency, Truman turned to more seasoned hands for advice. As Hardeman and Bacon put it, "Reaching out for all the help he could get, the new president was drawn closer to the plain-talking Texan."[24] When asked whether Truman would retain FDR's cabinet, Rayburn wrote, "How many of the resignations will be accepted by him or be replaced by folks of his liking, I do not know yet, but I will certainly give him the best counsel and advice possible."[25] Recounting his role to Martin Agronsky in 1958, Rayburn said that he warned Truman about the line of hangers-on, "sycophants," and special interests likely to seek the president's attention.[26]

Of course, after the transition, Rayburn's most important advice concerned the legislative process. Truman met weekly with Rayburn and other congressional leaders to go over legislative matters, their prospects for passage, and their policy implications.[27] Rayburn, along with his longtime friend Senate Majority Leader Alben Barkley of Kentucky and John McCormack, consulted regularly with Truman on party and legislative matters.[28]

Despite the experience and personal unity of this alliance, Truman's Seventy-Ninth Congress was viewed largely as lackluster, particularly in terms of its domestic policy output. When Truman sent a long list of legislative proposals after the end of World War II, Rayburn thought it overly ambitious and unlikely to pass as Truman had formulated the program.[29] Allied in 1946, Rayburn and Truman passed both the Legislative Reorganization Act and the Administrative Procedures Act, two pieces of legislation that were essential to help the structures of national government adjust to the drastic changes in Washington that resulted from New Deal gains and the impact of the war. But with the war concluded and in the wake of the domestic accomplishments of the New Deal, the Seventy-Ninth Congress's focus on stabilizing the international arena and building up the infrastructure of American national government seemed meager. It was, according to Hardeman and Bacon, "one of the least productive, most acrimonious sessions in years."[30] Moreover, these historic accomplishments did little to help the Democrats in the election. By September of 1946, Rayburn was aware that Democrats were in trouble and worried that Truman would have a Congress that was "destructive" and "swayed by partisanship," thus impeding needed progress.[31]

With the 1946 elections, Democrats lost control of the House, and Rayburn lost the Speakership to Republican Joe Martin. Just months into the Eightieth Congress, Truman delivered a speech to a Democratic "Jefferson Day Dinner" and referred to Rayburn, who was present, calling him "Mr. Speaker—to me you will always be Mr. Speaker."[32] But Rayburn was also a uniquely talented minority leader, marshaling votes to help Truman's foreign policy agenda and helping to build a case for a Democratic majority in 1948, including dubbing the Republican-controlled Eightieth Congress a "do-nothing Congress."

In the midst of his campaign for reelection and against the do-nothing Eightieth Congress, Truman took pains to exempt the Democrats, especially Rayburn:

> Now you have a bunch of wonderful men in the Congress, but they are in the minority, and when I speak of the 80th Congress—the 80th "do-nothing" Congress—I am talking about the leadership and majority control of that Congress. There never was a better man than Sam Rayburn in the Congress of the United States. If this country does what it ought to—and I am sure it is going to—Sam Rayburn will be the next Speaker of the House of Representatives.[33]

Campaigning through Texas on the back of a train in 1948, Truman asked voters not only to return him, but also the Democratic majority in the House so that he could "see Sam Rayburn sitting up in the Speaker's chair where he belongs"[34] and so that the Speaker would "have a powerful voice" that could provide "government in the interest of the farmer and the workingman and all the people."[35]

Publicly and privately, Truman celebrated Rayburn's value to the Congress and the country. So high was Truman's regard for Rayburn that he seriously thought about adding him to his own ticket in 1948 as vice president. Rayburn reportedly refused (as did Supreme Court Justice William O. Douglas) and then helped maneuver, seemingly against Truman's wishes, so that their mutual friend Alben Barkley would have the votes of a sufficient number of delegates to be nominated.[36] Anticipating a future Democratic House majority and Rayburn's return to the chair, Truman went on to advocate that the Speaker of the House (rather than Cabinet members or a Senate leader) be next in line for the presidency after the vice president in the Presidential Succession Act of 1947. This was widely taken as the ultimate confidence in Rayburn to provide steady leadership to the nation in time of great crisis.

Although they had their differences (Truman, Rayburn thought, "shot from the hip"[37]), Rayburn and Truman were close—personally and in political outlook. Rayburn had a high regard for his friend who had become president. Looking back, Rayburn said, "He made some of the greatest decisions that any president ever made and he made them with courage and stood by them, because Harry Truman is physically and morally a brave man."[38] Working hand in hand, these friends extended Franklin Roosevelt's legacy, legislated a successful rebuilding of Europe after World War II, and engaged in the massive government reorganizations necessary to accommodate the changes that the New Deal brought to Washington, DC. With Rayburn's support and advice, Truman's presidency was much more of a success than it might have been, given Truman's relative inexperience in operating at the highest level of governance.

## *Conflict and Compromise in Divided Government: Rayburn and Eisenhower*

Dwight Eisenhower's presidency cast Rayburn (along with Lyndon Johnson in the Senate) in the role of leader of the Democratic opposition. Prior to Eisenhower's election, Rayburn's Speakership had been devoted to delivering legislative accomplishments for Democratic administrations. Undoubtedly, Rayburn's patriotism and his political sense counseled cooperating with Eisenhower wherever possible, but Rayburn's commitment to the Democratic Party suggested that he also needed to defend his members and press the party's advantages wherever possible.

Scholars and other observers differ over the nature of the relationship between Eisenhower and Rayburn. Before his family relocated to Kansas, Ike had been born in Texas's Grayson County, adjacent to Rayburn's Fannin County, where his family had relocated after leaving Tennessee. Eisenhower had been born in Rayburn's district and referred to himself as a "vicarious constituent" of the Speaker. In many respects the president and Rayburn worked well together.[39] Looking back on the Eisenhower presidency, Rayburn himself observed,

> Eisenhower is the only man in history who was President of the United States eight years with the opposition party in control of both houses six of the eight years. So if we had been trying to make a failure out of him, he couldn't have done anything. But when he advocated something that we thought to be in the interest of the country, we supported him just as if there had been a Democrat in there.[40]

But this purported good will between the two masked as much as it revealed. Behind the scenes, Rayburn was expressing increasing frustration with Eisenhower's lack of political experience. The inability of the president to deliver conservative Republican votes on key legislative measures put pressure on Rayburn to "bail him out" in order to save administration initiatives.[41] From the beginning, Rayburn looked with suspicion on the neophyte leader. When Democrats approached Rayburn about a "draft Eisenhower" effort in 1948, Rayburn's opinion of Ike was "Good man but wrong business."[42]

Rayburn's business, by contrast, was legislating and politics. Having lost the White House for the first time in two decades, Rayburn (along with Lyndon Johnson) had to lead his party. Indeed, a chief task during the Eisenhower administration was, as minority leader, trying to rebuild the Democratic majority. Although Rayburn was typically a taciturn leader who thought it best to let disparate Democratic members campaign on their own terms and their own issues, the majority-building tasks of the 1954 election seemed to counsel a different approach. Contemporary reports suggested that "Rayburn will be coming out of the background and onto the floor more and more to emphasize views that will be important in November."[43] In addition to shaping a legislative record on which Democrats could run for election, Rayburn led criticism of the record of the Republican-controlled Eighty-Third Congress, which he called "dismal," and of the Eisenhower administration, which he thought "inept."[44] Even here, though, Rayburn recognized Eisenhower's personal popularity and approached criticism of the president carefully. In April of 1954, Rayburn said, "I expect the President wished he had run on the Democratic ticket," and he pledged to continue to work with the president on areas of agreement between Eisenhower and the Democrats—"to help Ike if it helps Democrats."[45]

If they were partisan rivals in 1954, the general view was that both men worked cooperatively together on legislation, especially on foreign policy. There is no doubt that Eisenhower preferred working with other officials, that is, constitutional officers, and thus would see more appropriateness in working with the Speaker than with other party leaders such as House floor leaders John McCormack and Joe Martin, whom he thought mere partisans. Still, even beyond election season, cooperation between Rayburn and Eisenhower would sometimes break down when the administration, often led by Vice President Nixon, took a more partisan tone. Sarah McClendon, whose questions to Eisenhower often indicated that she had a pipeline to Rayburn, posed the following question to Eisenhower in a press conference: "Mr. Sam Rayburn . . . told the House yesterday . . . the bipartisan foreign policy you want was threatened by the Nixon speech, and he sort of warned that if any more speeches came out like that, that hurt the Democrats' feelings very deeply, that there might not be any bipartisan foreign policy." Obviously irritated by the criticism, Ike responded, ". . . I am working for a proper, long-range, commonly supported foreign policy, and I am not going to give up just because someone may have hurt my feelings or threaten me or anything else."[46]

New to partisan politics, Eisenhower wished to be seen as above such squabbles and generally resisted public displays of pique at Rayburn. Rayburn reciprocated, and in one telling story, President Eisenhower recalled to his aides an unsolicited eruption of praise from Speaker Rayburn for his 1957 Second Inaugural Address. Eisenhower speechwriter Emmet John Hughes recalled: [47]

> [Ike] happily related, the morning after the Inaugural ceremonies, a distinguished friend's response. 'Sam Rayburn, my gosh, he almost embarrassed me yesterday,' [Ike] reported. 'He was so full of praise after the speech. He came up to me and said so seriously, 'I'd never say this publicly, and I'd never admit it to another Republican, but that was just the finest speech I've heard in forty-six years in this town.'

Eisenhower said this not only out of a sense of propriety but also an awareness that while he was personally popular, the public nevertheless still preferred Democrats to Republicans. Behind the scenes, though, Eisenhower occasionally communicated his disfavor. For example, Eisenhower conspicuously neglected to talk to Rayburn at a White House Correspondents Dinner after a parting of ways on a legislative matter.[48] Looking back, the highly partisan Republican leader Charles Halleck also noted that the Eisenhower-Rayburn relationship was more tense than was generally recognized. "I well remember that the then Speaker Sam Rayburn and the then majority leader in the Senate, Lyndon Johnson, were quite put out with President Eisenhower sometimes because of lack of consultation on appointments that had to go to Democrats."[49] Moreover, Halleck, who was charged with building Republican majorities in the House, threw cold water on the idea that Rayburn delivered votes for Eisenhower's legislative program:

> There was always that affinity of Texans and what have you . . . But the critical stuff, we didn't get any help from Sam Rayburn. Joe Martin would say at the meeting, you know, at the White House, 'Well I'll have a talk with Sam,' but, you know that was his way of doing. Well, I never could see where, if he had any such conversations that it meant a damned thing in the way of votes on the floor of the House.[50]

And after Halleck had ousted Martin as Republican leader, Halleck still believed that it was really up to the Republican leadership to deliver votes for Eisenhower: "I think probably he [Rayburn] could have been more active maybe and more aggressive against some of the things Eisenhower wanted," but Rayburn was unwilling to deliver votes "as far as getting the things through."[51]

Politically, Eisenhower had to tap dance around Rayburn, whose reputation was strong particularly because he muted his partisan tendencies. To avoid the partisan tone that might bring his public support down, Eisenhower's typical response to rumors of conflict aimed to downplay partisan difference and assert that he and Rayburn were close. When asked toward the end of his presidency if he was meeting more with Johnson than with Rayburn, Eisenhower's response was a mix of constitutional-formal and personal:

> The only time, I think, that you have to talk with the Leader of the Senate more than you do with the Speaker, is because you have the whole thing of confirmations and of treaties, and therefore a somewhat more intimate relationship to the whole business of foreign negotiation and activity. I think those would be the only places. And I must say, both these men, let's remember, are not only warm personal friends, but I think all of us have a common pride, understood by any other Texan, that we were all born in Texas. [Laughter] So I don't think there is any intimation whatsoever of differentiation, but it does happen in this one field you have more opportunities.[52]

Some sense of the increasing tension between the two men seemed to be getting out to the press and the broader public, however. By the end of his administration, Eisenhower had to deny reports of strain in the relationship. One question posed to the president during a 1959 press conference asked him about his "relations with the Democratic Congress" and "whether you are still finding time for an occasional visit with Speaker Rayburn and Senator Johnson, the two leaders in Congress." Eisenhower responded, "Now, so far as I know, there has been no damage to the personal relations between the three of us, and therefore there is no reason why we shouldn't have personal meetings. Now, when it comes down to the relations of any President with a Congress controlled by the opposite party, I just say this: it is no bed of roses."[53]

Even if Eisenhower was a popular president and a "vicarious constituent," Rayburn grew frustrated with the administration. Rayburn described Eisenhower's administration as "the most inept and blundering administration I have ever served with" and, of Eisenhower, Rayburn complained to aide D. B. Hardeman, "He can't find his ass with both hands."[54] There is no doubt that Eisenhower was a political neophyte as president, but one wonders, too, what else Rayburn, a staunch Democrat, would say about the only Republican president with whom he served as Speaker.

## *Master Mentor for the New Frontier: Rayburn and Kennedy*

John F. Kennedy was thirty-five years Rayburn's junior, and he was elected to the House of Representatives in 1946, a full thirty-three years after Rayburn first entered the House and six years after Rayburn had become Speaker. More than a generation senior to Kennedy, Rayburn had been on opposite sides in major party fights from JFK's politically powerful father, Joseph Kennedy, both in regard to Rayburn's support of John Nance Garner for the Democratic Presidential nomination in 1932 and in his displeasure at Joe Kennedy's being named by FDR as chairman of the Securities and Exchange Commission.[55] This decades-long rivalry could not have helped John Kennedy's reputation in the Speaker's eyes. In Rayburn's estimation, Kennedy was a new, inferior kind of congressman—more publicity-oriented, seemingly less policy-conscious, and less committed to the House as an institution than Rayburn preferred. Monumentally unimpressed by JFK during his six years in the House, Rayburn thought Kennedy a "showhorse" and a dilettante. The Speaker also resisted Kennedy's quasi-aristocratic roots and consequent arrogance and sense of entitlement. As close as Rayburn was to John McCormack, it is likely that the Boston rivalry between the Kennedy family and the McCormacks informed some of his antipathy, as well.

An early indication of the tension between the two men was that Rayburn worked against an effort to put Kennedy on the ballot as Adlai Stevenson's vice presidential running mate in 1956. Rayburn's lackluster support for Kennedy in 1956 should have been obvious to Massachusetts Democrat (and soon to be governor) Foster Furcolo when the Speaker wrote, "I have your letter with reference to your desire to see Senator John Kennedy the nominee for Vice-President. . . . I like John but we will just have to see what works out in Chicago."[56] Although there was much at work against Kennedy's candidacy, Kennedy came to believe that Rayburn was instrumental in denying him the vice presidential nomination in 1956, even joking after 1960 that he should thank Rayburn for saving his career and electability by blocking his candidacy on the ultimately failed 1956 ticket.

So widespread were the rumors that Rayburn was cool on Kennedy that some Kennedy supporters believed that it slowed the 1960 campaign. Stewart Udall, then a member of the House, said that he reached out to Kennedy's campaign to volunteer to help in the 1960 effort: "They never would have thought of recruiting me because most of the congressmen were cowed by Sam Rayburn. You know, unless you were from Massachusetts or unless you were a close personal friend of Jack Kennedy, very few of the congressmen stuck their necks out."[57]

There is no doubt that Rayburn had a preferred candidate in 1960—his protégé Lyndon Johnson—who, Rayburn believed, had the requisite experience and a string of legislative accomplishments that far outmatched Kennedy's record.

But, of course, Kennedy's political acumen and media style were well matched for the new politics that was emerging in the television age. Rayburn, a long-time admirer of political skill, developed respect for Kennedy, at least as a political leader, as time went on. Like much of America, Rayburn impressively took note of Kennedy's performance in the televised debates with Richard Nixon. No fan of Nixon, Rayburn said, "The Kennedy-Nixon debates have certainly shown the difference between the two and their alertness mentally. I am amazed at the wide knowledge Kennedy has of affairs, both domestically and foreign."[58] In the heat of the 1960 campaign, Rayburn wrote to Bob Poage, "I think Kennedy's trip through Texas was the best I have ever seen and I traveled part way through the state with President Roosevelt, all the way with President Truman, and most of the way with Adlai Stevenson. It seems to me that Kennedy has a great appeal, especially to the young folks and most of the women."[59]

Still, Rayburn's earlier views of Kennedy became an important part of the rumor mill concerning their relationship. When asked if the relationship between Rayburn and Kennedy had been "warm and friendly or still cool," Dick Bolling said that Rayburn had been "as against Kennedy as a human being can get. . . . But once the man was a nominee of the Democratic Party, Rayburn was for him, and he was for him—not just part for him—he was for him."[60] By the same token, Hale Boggs said, "After Mr. Kennedy was nominated for the presidency, nobody on earth campaigned harder for him than Sam Rayburn!"[61] By 1961, Rayburn was calling Kennedy "a young man of destiny," predicting that "he is going to make a great president."[62]

More than just a growing personal respect, Rayburn was probably more motivated by a sense of duty as Speaker to help the Democratic president achieve his legislative aims as well as his fervent hope to see his protégé LBJ succeed as well. Nowhere was this clearer than when the Speaker launched his historic battle in 1961 to expand the House Committee on Rules. Cautiously optimistic about Kennedy's legislative prospects, Rayburn said, "We must not look for miracles by the new Kennedy administration in the next 100 days. There is a lot of work to be done by all of us and I intend to give the new administration the tools it needs to get the work done. That's why I am convinced that this change in the Rules Committee is important."[63]

Even though the outcome of the Rules fight was essential to Kennedy's first-year success, the president quite wisely deferred to Rayburn's wishes that the administration keep the Rules fight at arms length and leave it to the House to determine the outcome. When asked about his potential role in a press conference, Kennedy acknowledged that "the Constitution states that each house shall be the judge of its own rules," and that Rayburn was "extremely anxious that the House be permitted to settle this matter in its own way."[64] Kennedy said, "The responsibility rests with the Members of the House, and I would not attempt in any way to infringe upon that responsibility" but, he joked, "I merely give my view as an interested citizen [Laughter]."[65] Once the fight was concluded and Rayburn was victorious, Kennedy was asked if the closeness of the vote signaled a weak legislative program; citing Rayburn's role in the victory, he acknowledged that all that was earned was a chance to be victorious legislatively:

> Well, the Speaker was successful yesterday and that does mean that the House will have an opportunity to vote on all these bills.
>
> I do think that the House is closely divided on a good many matters which involve legislative proposals, and perhaps the country may be divided, too, but at least we will have a chance to have a vote. And I consider that the most important thing. If the House then doesn't want to support our proposals then at least I feel that the country has indicated its judgment and not the judgment of only a small number of Representatives.[66]

After Rayburn won the Rules Committee fight, the path was cleared for much of the Kennedy program to receive votes on the House floor. If the expanded Rules Committee obstructed an education funding bill over questions related to aid to parochial schools, the rest of the program was passed on by Rules to the House in 1961. Dick Bolling, who was on the Rules Committee said, "We usually got a majority for what the president and the Speaker wanted, and they were together most of the time."[67] Kennedy was consultative, perhaps even to the surprise of the Speaker. Rayburn and other legislative leaders met with Kennedy every Tuesday morning. Of Kennedy, he said, "He doesn't take up all the time; he asks other people what they think."[68] For the most part, Kennedy had a good legislative year full of domestic policy accomplishments for his New Frontier that were due, in significant part, to Rayburn's procedural victory on the size of the Rules Committee.

Overall, Sam Rayburn came to approve of Kennedy as a man and as a Democratic leader. No longer simply a neophyte congressman who was a dilettante and a publicity seeker, Rayburn thought Kennedy had grown considerably. On one occasion in 1961, he said, "When the Kennedy administration makes a mistake, the president does not try to shift the blame to someone else—he stands up and takes the blame himself. He is a real man. That kind of responsibility makes for real leadership."[69] Looking back on the young president's first year, toward the very end of his life Rayburn said, "I think President Kennedy had one of the most successful sessions of Congress that I ever served in. In his State of the Union message, he laid down quite a program. Much of it was controversial. The Congress passed on every one of his proposals in some way, and the vast majority of them have been enacted into law."[70]

As is the case with most presidencies, Kennedy's first year was his best legislative year. But one could hardly call Kennedy's treatment by House Rules Committee Chair Howard Smith of Virginia and other conservative Democrats or the Republicans a "honeymoon." To the contrary, much of the credit for his legislative success is due to Rayburn's commitment to seeing the president succeed and the skill with which he was able to alter the Rules Committee to clear the path for the New Frontier. The fact that Congress acted on all of Kennedy's legislation was the real achievement, and because of Rayburn's work to expand the Rules Committee, credit for that fact goes to the Speaker. Without Rayburn after 1961, Kennedy's legislative success plummeted. And, of course, it would be Lyndon Johnson who would complete the Kennedy program after the president's assassination two years after Rayburn's death.

## *Conclusions*

When Sam Rayburn died in 1961, his accomplishments and legacy were already widely acknowledged. Honoring his memory, the three living presidents with whom he had served sang his praises. To Eisenhower, setting aside the interparty tensions that were part of their complex relationship, Rayburn "was a tower of strength for four presidents" when it came to "international affairs," and his "legislative leadership was unmatched."[71] Rayburn's friend Harry Truman called Mr. Sam "a statesman" and observed, "When history is written, he will appear as one of the very great men of this period."[72] As for sitting President Kennedy, who had come to rely on Rayburn's counsel and leadership in the first months of the New Frontier, Rayburn's "temperament and his character . . . were bedded in rock and remained unchanged by circumstance."[73] To be sure, Rayburn's experience and accomplishments must have seemed massive and daunting to the new young President:

> Mrs. Kennedy and I join the nation in mourning the death of Speaker Rayburn. His public service stretched from the administration of Woodrow Wilson to the present day. But it was the quality of that service more than its length that was so distinctive.
>
> A strong defender of constitutional responsibilities of the Congress, he had an instinctive understanding of the American system and was a loyal counselor and friend of Presidents of both parties on the great matters which affected our national interest and security.[74]

If one might expect such lavish public memorializing upon the death of an institution like Sam Rayburn, behind-the-scenes the assessments were even greater. If Truman's public statements celebrated Rayburn as "one of the very great men of this period," in a private letter to John McCormack, Truman offered that McCormack "had all the ability and experience to be a great Speaker" and compared McCormack's following Rayburn to his own experience succeeding to the Presidency, and following a great man, upon Roosevelt's death:

> Do you remember back in 1945 when President Franklin died and I was the next in line? Well I just went to work on the job. History will say whether I did it or not. I was not trying to be another Franklin Roosevelt. I had a job to do and did my damnedest. . . . Do the job as you see it and let 'em go to hell.[75]

Truman's comparison of following Rayburn to his own daunting historical role in following Roosevelt reveals the importance that key Washington insiders attributed to Rayburn's role as Speaker. For the middle part of the twentieth century, he was not only the most important member of the House of Representatives, but also the representative of the institution itself. At a point in American history when, because parties were weak and divided, we should expect a weak speakership,[76] Sam Rayburn stood out, enlarged the Speakership, and protected and advanced the role of the House of Representatives in the separation of powers. The most potent Speaker of the twentieth century, he was, to each of these presidents, the most formidable Speaker with whom they served, and they served with him as both ally and rival, depending on the fight at hand. This is a fact that Roosevelt, working with the fourth Speaker of his presidency, realized early on in his association with Rayburn. Two years into Rayburn's Speakership, Roosevelt wrote to him, "An important post always, the Speakership has assumed a special importance because of the gravity of the issues with which you have continually had to deal. Keep up the good work. The country has need of you."[77]

LIBRARY
WE THE PEOPLE

A picture of Rayburn's Tennessee home, hanging on the wall in Rayburn's Bonham home. *Photo by Melissa Baird Riddlesperger.*

8

# All Are Welcome

## *Sam Rayburn House and Museum: A Photo Essay*

Ashley Hodge
*Photographs by Melissa Baird Riddlesperger*

"Any jackass can kick down a barn, but it takes a good carpenter to build one, and we in Congress are in the business of carpentry."—Sam Rayburn

Born in Tennessee in 1882, Sam Rayburn moved to Texas as a child. Inspired to run for elected office at an early age, he was first elected to Congress in 1912, and after a distinguished career as a rank-and-file member of the House, he became Speaker in 1940. He served as Speaker of the United States House of Representatives for the longest tenure in history—seventeen years. When he relinquished that position in 1947 and became minority leader, he lost the use of the Speaker's limousine. Members of Congress were heartbroken to see their former Speaker without a car, so they made a plan to collect donations to purchase him a new Cadillac. Upon catching wind of the plan, Rayburn informed the congressman in charge that he had a personal stance against accepting gifts in excess of twenty-five dollars. With that in mind, the congressman collected twenty-five dollars from many different members of Congress and purchased the former Speaker a new 1947 Cadillac. This heartwarming story of admiration speaks to the influence Sam Rayburn had in Washington. As the second Speaker of the House from Texas, he worked endlessly to make Texas a player in

Rayburn's 1947 Cadillac parked in his garage.

national politics. His efforts paid off in Texas's influence in the nation's capital.

To fully understand the rich history that lies within the walls of Rayburn's home in Bonham, Texas, we must examine the history of the house itself. We will look at how the house and the man that inhabited it put Texas on the political map. Finally, to fully understand the impact that Sam Rayburn had on our state, we will examine how his legacy lives on today.

In 1914 Speaker Rayburn and his brother paid six thousand dollars to purchase 121 acres of land near Bonham, Texas. Rayburn once said, "The one thing besides people that I claim to know is land," and he proved this by building a farm that produced cotton, corn, and sorghum crops and provided pastureland for cattle. On this land, he built a charming two-story house from a Sears Roebuck kit that he continued to add on to for many years. Today, the house contains all of Rayburn's original furnishings. They remain where they were when

Rayburn paced his home thinking of ways to make Texas a force to be reckoned with.

The Speaker was only married for a brief time, and he never had children, but he was never alone in his home. He opened it to his family to live with him and grow with him as he moved through the ranks from congressman to Speaker. Beyond that, he shared it with the people of Bonham who were almost indistinguishable from his family. It was an attitude that extended to all of his constituents throughout his tenure in Washington.

Sam Rayburn was elected to the Texas House of Representatives in 1906. During his time as representative, he attended the University of Texas Law School and earned his law degree in 1908. While serving in the Texas House, he was elected its Speaker. Shortly after, in 1912,

Rayburn home, Bonham, Texas.

Desk in Rayburn's home where he greeted visiting guests.

he was elected as the Congressman from the Fourth Congressional District and served with President Woodrow Wilson. He remained a congressman for forty-nine years. In 1940, Sam Rayburn was elected Speaker of the US House, serving as Speaker when the Democrats were in power, and as minority leader when the Republicans had taken control of the House. During his time as Speaker, he oversaw the spread of electricity throughout the United States, and he was the chief congressional sponsor of the New Deal and the Fair Deal. James Riddlesperger has said that "[Rayburn] was a man who could say 'trust me,' and the answer among the representatives was 'yes, Mr. Sam.'" He proved this with arguably the most successful action he took during his time as Speaker: getting multimillion dollar appropriations approved by Congress without the representatives knowing what it was intended for—the top-secret Manhattan Project. Sam Rayburn ushered in the age of the New Deal and the age of nuclear power. His service in Congress spanned the Depression, World War II, the rise of the United States as a leading world power, and the beginning of the Civil Rights Era.

According to the Sam Rayburn House website, Rayburn said, "When I get away from Washington, I don't want to go anywhere in the world but home," and that is what he considered Bonham—home. When he wasn't working in Washington, he was home welcoming the people of Bonham through his back door; friends never used the front entrance. It is said that Sam Rayburn's favorite office was not on Capitol Hill, but rather in the sitting room of his home. He always took the time to listen to what his constituents had to say to ensure that he was

The back porch.

Dining room, Rayburn home.

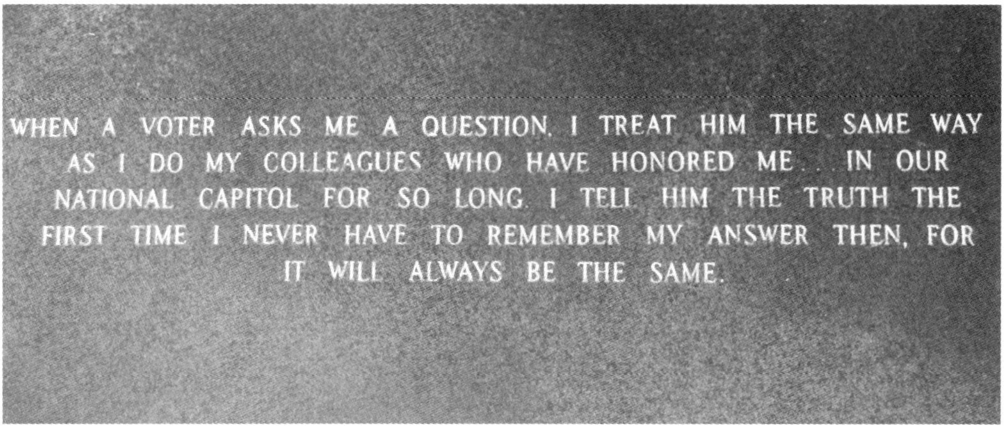

Rayburn quote engraved in stone in front of Rayburn Library.

providing for the people. Practices like this fueled Rayburn's legend.

The Speakership conveyed the unique opportunity for "Mr. Sam" to appoint representatives to congressional committees. Rayburn put a Texan on every major committee in Congress. He wanted to make sure that Texas "had fingers in every piece of the pie." Beyond this, each week, Speaker Rayburn had meetings with the delegates from Texas. Even weeks were social meetings in which everyone was invited. On odd weeks, the meetings were closed so that Texas delegates could discuss the finer details of their legislative efforts frankly and in private.

Like many Texans, Rayburn was a plain talker and a straight shooter. He knew that there was no point in beating around the bush on any occasion. He was quoted saying "I have found that people respect you if you tell them where you stand." Sam Rayburn was known for his fairness and integrity, and he made sure to treat the members of Congress with respect, no matter their political affiliation or views on particular topics of discussion. It is still said among members of Congress and those who knew him that his credibility was legendary. According to Riddlesperger, the Speaker was "universally respected as a man of integrity." Rayburn also played the important part of a mentor in more than one notable politician's life. Among his protégés were names such as Jim Wright, who also went on to become Speaker, and Lyndon B. Johnson, who became president in 1963.

Johnson portrait displayed in Rayburn's home.

Guest bedroom at Rayburn's home.

LBJ and his wife Lady Bird occasionally visited Rayburn's home and stayed in the lower floor guest bedroom.

Another of Rayburn's close friends was Harry Truman. Rayburn was having a drink with Truman when he received the call that Franklin Delano Roosevelt had died, making Truman the thirty-third president of the United States. Truman was scheduled to stay with Rayburn in the guest room during the presidential campaign of 1948, but plumbing problems in the house forced Truman instead to sleep on his campaign train.

Rayburn was able to relate to America's political elites as well as to small farmers. One can see that in how he dressed. When in Washington, he wore expensive tailor-made suits and shined shoes. Once he entered his district, however, he dressed informally, and was frequently seen wearing a white shirt with no tie or coat, khaki pants, and badly worn shoes. Though Rayburn was universally respected and could be avuncular with his colleagues, he could also be tough. According to Riddlesperger, "He could be mean as hell if you crossed him." Despite his temper, he sought to work with others. He took care of his own and he took care of his state.

"The greatest ambition a man can have is to be a just man," Rayburn once said. This statement speaks volumes to his character. He cared for others, but beyond anything, he cared for his constituents—his fellow Texans. Though a political figure of national influence, he also worked to ensure that Texas was a political force that had to be recognized on the national stage. Through examining the rich history of the Sam Rayburn House, the political influence he wielded, and the legacy he left behind, we have a much better understanding of how the Sam Rayburn House remains a metaphor for the best that Texas represents as a state. Speaker Rayburn was a great man, and he was a great Texan.

# Notes

## *Chapter 3*

1. C. Dwight Dorough, *Mr. Sam* (New York: Random House, 1962), pp. 75-121.

2. Ibid., p. 112.

3. Anthony Champagne, *Congressman Sam Rayburn* (New Brunswick: Rutgers University Press, 1984), pp. 97–103; Anthony Champagne, Douglas B. Harris, James W. Riddlesperger, and Garrison Nelson, *The Austin/Boston Connection: Five Decades of House Democratic Leadership, 1937–1989* (College Station: Texas A&M University Press, 2009), pp. 37–42.

4. Dorough, p. 119.

5. Champagne, *Congressman Sam Rayburn*, pp. 1–20.

6. Ibid., p. 14.

7. Ibid., pp. 16–17.

8. Allan Shivers interview with Anthony Champagne, August 13, 1984, Briscoe Center, Austin, Texas.

9. Champagne, *Congressman Sam Rayburn*, p. 17.

10. Ibid.

11. Ibid., p. 18.

12. Ibid.

13. 376 US 1 (1964).

14. Anthony Champagne, Douglas B. Harris, James W. Riddlesperger, and Garrison Nelson, *The Austin/Boston Connection: Five Decades of House Democratic Leadership, 1937–1989*, p. 59.

15. "Overview—Writing Democracy," www.writingdemocracy.weebly.com/overview.html.

16. Wright Patman interview by Joe B. Frantz, August 11, 1972, LBJ Library, pp. 5–6.

17. Anthony Champagne, "The Two Roles of Sam Rayburn," XX *East Texas Historical Journal* (1982), pp. 7–8.

18. D. B. Hardeman & Donald C. Bacon, *Rayburn: A Biography* (Austin: Texas Monthly Press, 1987), p. 202.

19. Ibid., pp. 202–203.

20. Edward Southerland, "Building Denison Dam," Texoma Living Online, August 5, 2010, www.texomaliving.com/denison-dam.

21. Ibid.

22. Jimmy Dale Puett, "Sam Rayburn's Influence on Public Policy" (MA thesis, East Texas State University, August, 1965), pp. 89–90.

23. Samuel Fenner Leslie, Interview with Wayne Little, July 26, 1965, Briscoe Center, Austin, Texas.

24. Ibid.

25. Paul Hardin, interview with Anthony Champagne, November 5, 1980, Briscoe Center, Austin, Texas.

26. Hardeman & Bacon, pp. 204–206, 298.

27. Champagne, "The Two Roles of Sam Rayburn," p. 8.

28. See generally, Valton J. Young, *The Speaker's Agent* (New York: Vantage, 1957)

29. Champagne, *Congressman Sam Rayburn*, p. 56.

30. Anthony Champagne, *Sam Rayburn: A Bio-Bibliography* (Westport, Conn.: Greenwood Press, 1988), p. 35.

31. Champagne, *Congressman Sam Rayburn*, p. 54; Paul J. Kilday, interview with H. W. Kamp, August 28, 1965, University of North Texas, Denton, Texas.

32. Champagne, *Congressman Sam Rayburn*, pp. 55–56

33. Truitt Smith, interview with Anthony Champagne, May 16, 1980, Briscoe Center, Austin, Texas.

34. Champagne, *Congressman Sam Rayburn*, p. 28.

35. Anthony Champagne, *Sam Rayburn: A Bio-Bibliography*, p. 34.

36. Champagne, *Congressman Sam Rayburn*, p. 32.

37. Champagne, *Congressman Sam Rayburn*, p. 34.

38. H. G. Dulaney, interview with Anthony Champagne, August 15, 1980 and R. C. Slagle, interview with Anthony Champagne, October 17, 1980, Briscoe Center, Austin, Texas.

39. Anthony Champagne, *Congressman Sam Rayburn*, p. 47.

40. Hardeman & Bacon, pp. 332–333.

41. Ibid., p. 332.

42. Ralph Hall speech, Friends of Sam Rayburn Barbecue, Bonham, Texas, June 13, 1981.

43. Robert Bradshaw, interview with Anthony Champagne, May 11, 1981, Briscoe Center, Austin, Texas.

44. Roland Boyd, interview with Anthony Champagne, May 22, 1980, Briscoe Center, Austin, Texas.

45. H. G. Dulaney, interview.

46. Ibid.

47. Champagne, *Congressman Sam Rayburn*, pp. 65–94.

## *Chapter 4*

1. D. Clayton Brown, *Electricity for Rural America: The Fight for the REA* (Westport, Connecticut, 1980), p. 61.

2. Ibid., p. 64.

3. Ibid., p. 64.

4. Ibid., p. 65.

5. D. Clayton Brown, "Sam Rayburn and the Development of Public Power in the Southwest," *Southwestern Historical Quarterly*, Vol. 73, (October 1974), p. 140.

6. Ibid., p. 142.

7. Ibid., p. 145.

8. Ibid., p.149.

9. D. Clayton Brown, "Sam Rayburn" in *Profiles in Power: Twentieth Century Texans in Washington*, edited by Kenneth E. Hendrickson and Michael L. Collins, (Arlington Heights, Illinois, 1993), p. 105.

## *Chapter 5*

1. James W. Riddlesperger, Jr. and Anthony Champagne, *Lone Star Leaders: Power and Personality in the Texas Congressional Delegation,* (Fort Worth: TCU Press, 2011), p. 12; Anthony Champagne, Douglas B. Harris, James W. Riddlesperger, Jr., and Garrison Nelson, *The Austin/Boston Connection,* (College Station: Texas A&M Press, 2009), p. 31.

2. Riddlesperger and Champagne, pp. 34–35.

3. Alfred Steinberg, *Sam Rayburn: A Biography,* (New York: Hawthorne, 1975), p. 225.

4. Tip O'Neill with William Novak, *Man of the House,* (New York: Random House, 1987), p. 127; Jim Wright, *Balance of Power,* (Atlanta: Turner Publishing, 1996), p.17.

5. Robert Dallek, *Lone Star Rising,* (New York: Oxford, 1991), p. 366.

6. D. B. Hardeman and Donald C. Bacon, (Austin: Texas Monthly Press, 1987), p. 306.

7. Anthony Champagne, *Congressman Sam Rayburn,*(New Brunswick, NJ: Rutgers, 1984), p. 38.

8. Wright, p. 55.

9. Transcript, James C. Wright, Jr. Oral History Interview I, 6/30/1969, by Joe B. Frantz, Lyndon Baines Johnson Library. p. 24.

10. Wright Oral History Interview, LBJ Library, p. 23.

11. James W. Riddlesperger, Jr. and Joanne Connor Green, "Texans in Congress: The Changing Nature of the Texas Congressional Delegation" in Anthony Champagne and Edward J. Harpham, eds., *Texas Politics: A Reader,* 2nd Edition, (New York: Norton, 1998), p. 39.

12. Randall, B. Woods, *LBJ: Architect of American Ambition,* (New York: Free Press, 2006), p. 160; Robert Dallek, *Lone Star Rising,* (New York: Oxford), p. 227;

Irwin Unger and Debi Unger, *LBJ: A Life*, (New York: John Wiley, 1999), p. 106; Alfred Steinberg, *Sam Johnson's Boy*, (New York: Macmillan, 1968), p. 186.

13. Wright Oral History Interview, LBJ Library, pp. 19-20.

14. Wright, p. 17.

15. O'Neill, p. 130.

16. James W. Riddlesperger, Jr., Anthony Champagne, and Dan Williams, eds., *The Wright Stuff: Reflections on People and Politics by Former House Speaker Jim Wright,* (Fort Worth: TCU Press, 2013), p. 17.

17. Woods, *LBJ*, p. 127.

18. Dallek, p. 166.

19. Woods, p. 131.

20. Booth Mooney, *The Politicians, 1945–1970,* (New York: Lippincott, 1970), p. 226.

21. Hardeman and Bacon, p. 390

22. O'Neill, p. 131.

23. Jim Wright, *Balance of Power*, (Atlanta: Turner Publishing, 1996), p. 17.

24. Author interview with Paul Driskell, October 7, 2015.

## *Chapter 6*

1. A fourth (and ancillary) House Office Building is named for former Republican House leader and former President Gerald Ford.

2. See David W. Rohde, *Parties and Leaders in the Postreform House* (Chicago: University of Chicago Press, 1991); Barbara Sinclair, *Legislators, Leaders and Lawmaking: The U.S. House of Representatives in the Postreform Era* (Baltimore: Johns Hopkins University Press, 1995); John H. Aldrich and David W. Rohde, "The Transition to Republican Rule: Implications for Theories of Congressional Politics" *Political Science Quarterly* 112:4 (1997–1998): 541–567.

3. Joseph Cooper and David W. Brady, "Institutional Context and Leadership Style: The House from Cannon to Rayburn" *American Political Science Review* 75 (1981): 411–425, p. 423.

4. See Rohde, *Parties and Leaders in the Postreform House*; Aldrich and Rohde, "Transitions to Republican Rule."

5. Elaine K. Swift, "The Start of Something New: Clay, Stevenson, Polk and the Development of the Speakership, 1789-1869." In Roger H. Davidson, Susan Webb Hammond, and Raymond W. Smock, eds., *Masters of the House: Congressional Leaders Over Two Centuries* (Boulder, CO: Westview Press, 1998), pp. 10–32.

6. Matthew N. Green, *The Speaker of the House: A Study of Leadership* (New Haven: Yale University Press, 2010).

7. Green examines Rayburn's role in, among other legislative battles, Draft Extension in 1941 as well as the Natural Gas Act in 1949, 1950, and 1955; *The Speaker of the House.*

8. Ronald M. Peters, Jr. and Cindy Simon Rosenthal, *Speaker Nancy Pelosi and the New American Politics* (New York: Oxford University Press, 2010).

9. Randall Strahan, *Leading Representatives: The Agency of Leaders in the Politics of the U.S. House* (Baltimore: Johns Hopkins University Press, 2007).

10. Indeed, Evans and Oleszek's work is a good example of how to situate leaders and their (to a degree) independent contributions into multiple contextual frameworks; C. Lawrence Evans and Walter J. Oleszek, "The Strategic Context of Congressional Leadership." *Congress & the Presidency* 26 (1999): 1-20; see also Douglas B. Harris, "House Majority Party Leaders' Uses of Public Opinion Information" *Congress & the Presidency* 32 (2005): 133–55.

11. Cooper and Brady, "Institutional Context and Leadership Style," p. 420; learning and other elements of the "supply side" of institutional change are considered in Lawrence C. Dodd, "Political Learning and Political Change: Understanding Development Across Time." In Lawrence C. Dodd and Calvin Jillson, eds., *The Dynamics of American Politics: Approaches and Interpretations* (Boulder, CO: Westview Press, 1994), pp. 331-364; Elaine K. Swift, *The Making of an American Senate: Reconstitutive Change in Congress, 1787-1841* (Ann Arbor: University of Michigan Press, 1996); Adam Sheingate, "Political Entrepreneurship, Institutional Change, and American Political Development" *Studies in American Political Development* 17:2 (2003): 185-203.

12. Joseph Cooper and Gary Bombardier, "Presidential Leadership and Party Success" *Journal of Politics* 30:4 (1968): 1012-1027; Cooper and Brady, "Institutional Context and Leadership Style."

13. Carl Albert (with Danney Goble), *Little Giant: The Life and Times of Speaker Carl Albert* (Norman: University of Oklahoma Press, 1990), p. 202.

14. Cooper and Brady, "Institutional Context and Leadership Style," p. 417.

15. Cooper and Brady, "Institutional Context and Leadership Style," p. 417.

16. Cooper and Brady, "Institutional Context and Leadership Style," p. 419-20.

17. Anthony Champagne, *Congressman Sam Rayburn* (New Brunswick: Rutgers University Press, 1984), p. 155.

18. Champagne, *Congressman Sam Rayburn*, pp. 155 6.

19. Neil MacNeil, *Forge of Democracy: The House of Representatives* (New York: David McKay, 1963), p. 83.

20. Quoted in Alvin M. Josephy, *On the Hill: A History of the American Congress* (New York: Simon and Shuster, 1979), p. 339

21. F. Edward Wood, Jr., 1968, 25.

22. Hardeman and Bacon, 307

23. Quoted in Champagne, *Congressman Sam Rayburn*, p. 155

24. Hardeman and Bacon, 308.

25. Indeed, Wood suggests that Rayburn's "taciturnity" was a part of his communications strategy in that Rayburn collected but rarely disseminated information; "being easy to contact but not effusive, it can be well imagined that a net flow of information toward Rayburn would be encouraged," p. 54.

26. Wood, p. 52.

27. See House Democratic Caucus, *http://www.dems.gov/about/*, accessed July 29, 2015; see, too, Matthew N. Green, "Institutional Change, Party Discipline and

the House Democratic Caucus, 1911–1919" *Legislative Studies Quarterly* 27 (2002): 601–33.

28. Hardeman and Bacon, *Rayburn*, p. 346.

29. Booth Mooney, *Mr. Speaker: Four Men Who Shaped the United States House of Representatives* (Chicago: Follett, 1964), p. 132.

30. Rayburn's search for and cultivation of bargaining chips is a good exemplar of one principle suggested in Cox and McCubbins's (1993) view of congressional leaders as solutions to the collective action problems of congressional majorities. Cox and McCubbins write: "consider a . . . model in which 1) everyone in [faction] *N* wants a bill, N, whose characteristics are common knowledge; 2) everyone in *N* (and *S*) thinks that there probably exists some sweetener S that will induce *S* to go along with them; but 3) no one knows exactly what this sweetener is; and 4) it would be costly to 'invent' an appropriate sweetener and sell it to *S* (and *N*). In this model, a free-rider problem arises for the members of *N* (and *S*): no single one of them wishes to bear or contribute to the costs of searching for the sweetener, because this action is invisible to voters and they cannot credibly claim credit for it;" Gary W. Cox and Mathew D. McCubbins, *Legislative Leviathan: Party Government in the House* (Berkeley: University of California Press, 1993), p. 125. As an example of the myriad collective action problems that arise in legislative settings to which Cox and McCubbins propose congressional leaders are the solution, this also closely mirrors Speaker Rayburn's cultivation of bargaining chips recounted below.

31. This is not to say that only bargaining era speakers accrue such resources; indeed, Cannon's speakership was noted for the power such accumulated favors could produce; see Cooper and Brady, "Institutional Context and Leadership Style," p. 413. Still, in the absence of strong intra-party unity and the formal mechanisms of party control of Cannon's "czar" era, Rayburn and other "bargaining" era speakers had to rely all the more on accumulated bargaining chips in order to be effective.

32. Tip O'Neill (with William Novak), *Man of the House: The Life and Political Memoirs of Speaker Tip O'Neill* (New York: Random House, 1987), p. 135.

33. O'Neill, *Man of the House*, p. 132.

34. MacNeil, *Forge of Democracy*.

35. I thank Joseph Cooper for sharing this observation with me.

36. Richard Bolling, *House Out of Order* (New York: Dutton, 1965), p. 65.

37. Clapp 1963, 325.

38. Clapp 1963, 326

39. Strahan, *Leading Representatives*, p. 3.

40. See Robert C. Lieberman, "Ideas, Institutions and Political Order: Explaining Institutional Change" *American Political Science Review* 96:4 (2002): 697–712, p. 703.

41. Gerald Gamm and Kenneth Shepsle, "Emergence of Legislative Institutions: Standing Committees in the House and Senate, 1810–1825" *Legislative Studies Quarterly* 14:1 (1989): 39-66; Randall Strahan, Vincent Moscardelli, Moshe

Haspel and Richard Wike, "The Clay Speakership Revisited" *Polity* 32:4 (2000): 561–93.

42. Hardeman and Bacon, *Rayburn: A Biography*, p. 119.

43. Hardeman and Bacon, *Rayburn: A Biography*, p. 119.

44. Hardeman and Bacon, *Rayburn: A Biography*, p. 119.

45. C. Dwight Dorough, *Mr. Sam* (New York: Random House, 1962), p. 385.

46. Hardeman and Bacon, *Rayburn: A Biography*, p. 5.

47. Bolling, *House Out of Order*, p. 153.

48. Dorough, *Mr. Sam*, p. 517.

49. H. G. Dulaney and Edward Hake Phillips, eds., *Speak, Mister Speaker* (Bonham, TX: Sam Rayburn Foundation, 1978), p. 459; quoted also in Dorough, *Mr. Sam*, p. 516.

50. Quoted in Dulaney and Phillips, *Speak, Mister Speaker*, p. 459.

51. Speaker Sam Rayburn to Robert Bartley 12/10/51. Quoted in Dulaney and Phillips, *Speak, Mister Speaker*, p. 202.

52. Hardeman and Bacon, *Rayburn: A Biography*, 425.

53. Dorough, *Mr. Sam*, p. 517.

54. Mooney, *Mr. Speaker*, p. 179.

55. Bolling, *House Out of Order*, p. 212.

56. William R. MacKaye, "A New Coalition Takes Control: The House Rules Committee Fight of 1961." *Eagleton Institute Cases in Practical Politics* 29 (New Brunswick: Rutgers University Press, 1963); Hardeman and Bacon, *Rayburn: A Biography*.

57. Milton C. Cummings, Jr. and Robert L. Peabody, "The Decision to Enlarge the Committee on Rules: An Analysis of the 1961 Vote." In Robert L. Peabody and Nelson W. Polsby eds., *New Perspectives on the House of Representatives* 2nd edition. (Chicago: Rand McNally, 1969), p. 263.

58. *Congressional Record*, January 31, 1961, pp. 1508–1510; cited in *Speak, Mister Speaker*, p. 429.

59. Peabody and Cummings, "The Decision to Enlarge the Committee on Rules," p. 279.

60. Douglas B. Harris, "The Rise of the Public Speakership" *Political Science Quarterly* 113 (1998): 193–212.

## *Chapter 7*

1. For four of these 21 years, the Democrats lost the majority in the House of Representatives, first during the th Congress during the Truman administration and then again during the Eighty-Third Congress, the first two years of the Eisenhower administration. During this four years, Rayburn served as the Democratic (minority) floor leader. The authors gratefully acknowledge the research assistance of undergraduate Zoe Kempf-Harris and the archivists of the papers of Speaker John W. McCormack in the Howard Gottlieb Archival Research Center at Boston University, Boston, Massachusetts.

2. See Anthony Champagne, Douglas B. Harris, James W. Riddlesperger, Jr., and Garrison Nelson, *The Austin-Boston Connection: Five Decades of House Democratic Leadership, 1937–1989* (College Station, TX: Texas A&M University Press, 2009); Douglas B. Harris, "Dwight Eisenhower and the New Deal: The Politics of Preemption" *Presidential Studies Quarterly* 27 (1997): 333–342.

3. See for example Lewis L. Gould and Nancy Beck Young, "The Speaker and the Presidents: Sam Rayburn, the White House, and the Legislative Process, 1941–1961." In Roger H. Davidson, Susan Webb Hammond, and Raymond W. Smock, eds., *Masters of the House* (Boulder, CO: Westview Press, 1998).

4. Joseph Cooper and David W. Brady, "Institutional Context and Leadership Style: The House from Cannon to Rayburn" 75 (1981): 411–425; F. Edward Wood, Johns Hopkins MA Thesis, 1968.

5. Richard Bolling, recorded interview by Richard J. Grele, November 1, 1965, 38, John F. Kennedy Library Oral History Program. https://archive2.jfklibrary.org/JFKOH/Boling,%20Richard%20W/JFKOH-RWB-01/JFKOH-RWB-01TR.pdf.

6. Hardeman and Bacon, *Rayburn*, p. 201.

7. Hardeman and Bacon, 207.

8. Champagne, Harris, Riddlesperger, and Nelson, *The Austin-Boston Connection*, 106–112.

9. Sam Rayburn, "The Speaker Speaks of Presidents" *New York Times*, June 4, 1961, 32.

10. John W. McCormack, recorded interview by Sheldon Stern, March 30, 1977, 16, John F. Kennedy Library Oral History Program.

11. Sam Rayburn, "The Speaker Speaks of Presidents" *New York Times*, June 4, 1961, 32.

12. Richard W. Bolling, oral history interview conducted by Niel M. Johnson, October 21, 1988, p. 115, Harry S. Truman Library & Museum, *http://www.trumanlibrary.org/oralhist/bolling.htm*, accessed September 19, 2015.

13. Franklin D. Roosevelt to Sam Rayburn, December 23, 1940, quoted in Booth Mooney, *Roosevelt and Rayburn: A Political Partnership* (Philadelphia: J.B. Lippincott, 1971), pp. 153–154.

14. Sidney M. Milkis, *Political Parties and Constitutional Government: Remaking American Democracy* (Baltimore: Johns Hopkins University Press, 1999), pp. 86-100.

15. Champagne, Harris, Riddlesperger, and Nelson, *The Austin-Boston Connection*, pp. 256–7.

16. Hardeman and Bacon, 277.

17. Conrad Black, *Franklin Delano Roosevelt, Champion of Freedom* (New York: Public Affairs, 2003), p. 656.

18. Hardeman and Bacon, 279.

19. Hardeman and Bacon, 279-80; Alfred Steinberg, *Sam Rayburn: A Biography* (New York: Hawthorn Books, 1975), 212; C. Dwight Dorough, *Mr. Sam* (New York: Random House, 1962), 371–372.

20. Hardeman and Bacon, *Rayburn*, 296–7.

21. Dorough, *Mr. Sam*, p. 353.

22. Harry S. Truman, "Rear Platform and Other Informal Remarks in Texas, September 23, 1948, [11.] Bells, Texas," in *Public Papers of the Presidents of the United States: Harry S. Truman, 1948,* 212 (Washington, DC: Government Printing Office, 1964), 591.

23. Harry S. Truman, "Rear Platform and Other Informal Remarks in Texas, September 27, 1948, [2.] Austin, Texas," in *Public Papers of the Presidents of the United States: Harry S. Truman, 1948,* 212 *Washington DC: Government Printing Office, 1964),* 581.

24. Hardeman and Bacon, *Rayburn*, p. 312.

25. Sam Rayburn letter dated April 27, 1945, in H. G. Dulaney and Edward Hake Phillips, *Speak, Mister Speaker* (Bonham, TX: Sam Rayburn Foundation, 1978), p. 122.

26. Sam Rayburn interview with Martin Agronsky, 1958, quoted in Dulaney and Phillips, *Speak, Mister Speaker*, p. 122–3.

27. Steinberg, *Sam Rayburn*, 230.

28. Rayburn and Barkley entered the House in 1913 and served together on the Interstate and Foreign Commerce Committee, with Rayburn being technically right behind Barkley in seniority. Indeed, it was Barkley's decision to move to the Senate that cleared the path for Rayburn to chair the committee before ascending to the Majority Leader's post; see David T. Canon, Garrison Nelson, and Charles Stewart III, *Committees in the U.S. Congress, 1789–1946: House Standing Committees* (Washington, DC: CQ Press,2002), pp. 625–627.

29. Steinberg, *Sam Rayburn: A Biography*, p. 233.

30. Hardeman and Bacon, *Rayburn*, p. 319.

31. Rayburn letter, September 3, 1946, in Dulaney and Phillips, *Speak, Mister Speaker*, p. 134.

32. Harry S. Truman, "Address at the Jefferson Day Dinner, April 5, 1947," in *Public Papers of the Presidents of the United States: Harry S. Truman, 1947,* 68 (Washington, DC: Government Printing Office, 1963), 192.

33. Harry S. Truman, "Rear Platform and Other Informal Remarks in Texas, September 28, 1948, [1.] Sherman, Texas," in *Public Papers of the Presidents of the United States: Harry S. Truman, 1948,* 213 (Washington, DC: Government Printing Office, 1964), 597.

34. Harry S. Truman, "Address at Bonham, Texas, September 27, 1948," in *Public Papers of the Presidents of the United States: Harry S. Truman, 1948,* 214 (Washington, DC: Government Printing Office, 1964), 596.

35. Harry S. Truman, "Address at Bonham, Texas, September 27, 1948," in *Public Papers of the Presidents of the United States: Harry S. Truman, 1948,* 213 (Washington, DC: Government Printing Office, 1964), 593.

36. Steinberg, *Sam Rayburn*, p. 243. Truman's opposition to Barkley, it seems, had more to do with his advanced age than with any lack of confidence.

37. C. Dwight Dorough, *Mr. Sam* (New York: Random House, 1962), p. 449.

38. Dorough, *Mr. Sam*, p. 448.

39. Dwight D. Eisenhower "Remarks at a Dinner Given by the Indiana State Society in Honor of Minority Leader Charles A. Halleck March 10, 1960," in *Public Papers of the Presidents of the United States: Dwight D. Eisenhower, 1960–61,* 88, Washington, DC: Government Printing Office, 1961), 287.

40. Sam Rayburn, "The Speaker Speaks of Presidents" *New York Times,* June 4, 1961, 32.

41. Hardeman and Bacon, *Rayburn: A Biography,* p. 378.

42. Steinberg, *Sam Rayburn: A Biography,* p. 242.

43. *U.S. News and World Report,* April 23, 1954, p. 12

44. *Congressional Quarterly Weekly Report,* September 3, 1954; and *U.S. News and World Report,* September 3, 1954.

45. *Congressional Quarterly Weekly Report,* May 28, 1954; *U.S. News and World Report,* January 8, 1954. For more extended treatment of Rayburn's role vis-à-vis Eisenhower in the 1954 election, see Douglas B. Harris, *The Public Speakership: Media and Party Leadership in the House of Representatives, 1950–1996* (PhD Dissertation, Johns Hopkins University, 1998), pp. 231–235.

46. Dwight D. Eisenhower, "The President's News Conference of June 30, 1954," in *Public Papers of the Presidents of the United States: Dwight D. Eisenhower, 1954,* 157 (Washington, DC: Government Printing Office, 1960), 613–614.

47. Emmet John Hughes, *The Ordeal of Power: A Political Memoir of the Eisenhower Years* (New York: Atheneum, 1962), pp. 231–232.

48. Dorough, *Mr. Sam,* 478-9.

49. Charles A. Halleck, recorded interview by Stephen Hess, March 22, 1965, 36, John F. Kennedy Library Oral History Program, https://archive1.jfklibrary.org/JFKOH/Halleck,%20Charles%20A/JFKOH-CAH-01/JFKOH-CAH-01-TR.pdf.

50. Charles Halleck, Oral History Interview by Thomas Soapes, April 26, 1977, Dwight D. Eisenhower Library, p. 29, http://www.eisenhower.archives.gov/research/oral_histories/oral_history_transcripts/Halleck_Cha rles_489.pdf.

51. Charles Halleck, Oral History Interview by Thomas Soapes, April 26, 1977, Dwight D. Eisenhower Library, p. 29, http://www.eisenhower.archives.gov/research/oral_histories/oral_history_transcripts/Halleck_Charles_489.pdf.

52. Dwight D. Eisenhower, "The President's News Conference of February 25, 1959," in *Public Papers of the Presidents of the United States: Dwight D. Eisenhower, 1959,* 42 (Washington, DC: Government Printing Office, 1960), 213.

53. Dwight D. Eisenhower, "The President's News Conference of July 14, 1959," in *Public Papers of the Presidents of the United States: Dwight D. Eisenhower, 1959,* 160 (Washington, DC: Government Printing Office, 1960), 523.

54. Quoted in Hardeman and Bacon, *Rayburn: A Biography,* p. 379.

55. Steinberg, *Sam Rayburn,* p. 118.

56. Rayburn to Foster Furcolo, August 6, 1956, in Dulaney and Phillips, *Speak, Mister Speaker,* p. 297.

57. Stewart L. Udall, recorded interview by W. W. Moss, January 12, 1970, 8, John F. Kennedy Library Oral History Program, https://archive2.jfklibrary.org/JFKOH/Udall,%20Stewart%20L/JFKOH-SLU-01/JFKOH-SLU-01-TR.pdf.

58. Quoted in Dulaney and Phillips, *Speak, Mister Speaker*, p. 414.

59. Rayburn to Poage, September 19, 1960, in Dulaney and Phillips, *Speak, Mister Speaker*, p. 412.

60. Richard Bolling, recorded interview by Richard J. Grele, November 1, 1965, 36–37, John F. Kennedy Library Oral History Program, https://archive2.jfklibrary.org/JFKOH/Bolling,%20Richard%20W/JFKOH-RWB-01/JFKOH-RWB-01-TR.pdf.

61. Hale Boggs, recorded interview by Charles T. Morrissey, May 10, 1964, 5, John F. Kennedy Library Oral History Program, https://archive2.jfklibrary.org/JFKOH/Boggs,&20Thomas%20Hale/JFKOH-THB-01/JFKOH-THB-10-TR.pdf.

62. Quoted in Dulaney and Phillips, *Speak, Mister Speaker*, p. 431.

63. Quoted in Dulaney and Phillips, *Speak, Mister Speaker*, p. 429.

64. John F. Kennedy, "The President's News Conference of January 25, 1961," in *Public Papers of the Presidents of the United States: John F. Kennedy, 1961*, 8, (Washington, DC: Government Printing Office, 1962), 11.

65. Kennedy, "The President's News Conference of January 25, 1961," 11.

66. John F. Kennedy, "The President's News Conference of February 1, 1961," in *Public Papers of the Presidents of the United States: John F. Kennedy, 1961*, 15, (Washington, DC: Government Printing Office, 1962), 35.

67. Richard Bolling, recorded interview by Richard J. Grele, November 1, 1965, 44, John F. Kennedy Library Oral History Program, https://archive2.jfklibrary.org/JFKOH/Bolling,%20Richard%20W/JFKOH-RWB-01?JFKOH-RWB-01-TR.pdf.

68. Quoted in Dulaney and Phillips, *Speak, Mr. Speaker*, 435.

69. Quoted in Dulaney and Phillips, *Speak, Mister Speaker*, 440.

70. Quoted in Dulaney and Phillips, *Speak, Mister Speaker*, 450.

71. "Leaders of Both Parties Join in Paying Tribute to Rayburn" *New York Times*, November 17, 1961.

72. "Leaders of Both Parties Join in Paying Tribute to Rayburn" *New York Times*, November 17, 1961.

73. John F. Kennedy, "Statement by the President on the Death of Sam Rayburn, November 16, 1961," in *Public Papers of the Presidents of the United States: John F. Kennedy, 1961*, 471 (Washington, DC: Government Printing Office, 1962), 724.

74. Kennedy, "Statement by the President on the Death of Sam Rayburn, November 16, 1961," 724.

75. Harry S. Truman to John McCormack, January 8, 1962, Folder "Spellman Letter" Box 194, the papers of Speaker John W. McCormack in the Howard Gotlieb Archival Research Center of Boston University, Boston, Massachusetts.

76. See Joseph Cooper and David W. Brady, "Institutional Context and Leadership Style: The House from Cannon to Rayburn" *American Political Science Review* 1981: 411–425.

77. Roosevelt to Rayburn, quoted in Booth Mooney, *Roosevelt and Rayburn*, p. 189.

# Index